Every mom should feast on this book of helpful ... *her life with all the varying responsibilities tha* ... *with solid, commonsense advice in easily digestible bites that give wholesome nutrition to every mother's soul. It's a perfect daily snack to be picked up, reflected upon, and reread. This book reinforces your good intentions to resist unhealthy stressors, to be kind to yourself, and to maintain equilibrium."*

—Robert J. Hudson, MD, FAAP, pediatrician and clinical professor of pediatrics at the University of Oklahoma School of Medicine

Many mothers live a life of frenzy trying to keep up with the schedules of their overly programmed children. Bria Simpson's book deals with these issues in an intelligent and practical manner. She correctly points out that the constant activity is also difficult for the children. One of my grandchildren, then nine years old, said to me that he wished he had a day with nothing to do. In relating that comment to a friend who happens to be a minister, he reflected that a day of rest is not a new idea. It is called the Sabbath.

—Steven Adelson, MD, pediatrician in private practice in Tulsa, OK

Entitlement is the key to feeling good about doing for ourselves—only then are we free to enjoy the role of caretaker. Bria Simpson's The Balanced Mom *gives women (with or without kids!) the permission to feel entitled in an easy-to-read format. I would wholeheartedly recommend this books to the moms I work with!*

—Julie Peters, Ph.D., licensed psychologist specializing in women's health and post-partum depression and mother of a toddler and a newborn

In this fast-paced world, where moms often feel the unnecessary pressure of perfection, The Balanced Mom *gives permission to moms to ditch the guilt of unrealistic expectations and start living a more authentic and fulfilling life. Bria Simpson's wit, passion, and life experiences shine through to inspire moms to proactively take the steps necessary to achieve this goal.*

—Katherine C. Holman, Ph.D., CCC-SLP, director of community outreach and training at the Center for Autism and Related Disorders of the Kennedy Krieger Institute and research faculty in the Department of Child and Adolescent Psychiatry at Johns Hopkins School of Medicine

This is one of the best books I've read! The Balanced Mom *is so easy to read with bite sized parenting wisdom that can be digested in minutes. Each perspective and tip is excellently written and right on track. Bria Simpson give moms a new mantra to separate what must be done from the absurd standards we hold ourselves to: will this matter in a year from now*

—Rhonda Hess, author, coach trainer, and president of Bubbling Well, Inc., a support provider to professional coaches for building financially successful businesses

Bria's insight into motherhood and its challenges always seems to speak to the situation at hand. Not only does she take a very realistic approach to the everyday stresses of being a mom, but also a very holistic one.

—Margie Warren, philanthropist and mother of three

Bria makes clear what can seem quite complicated and elusive—how to live a full and happy life as a mom! She does this without judgment, without scolding or artificially upholding one doctrine of living. She simply presents clear choices and thoughtful options that can help anyone realize the right path for them. She puts into perspective the choices that we can all make feel more fulfilled and happy. With Bria's help, I've seen the potential in my life despite the challenges of being a full-time working mother of two boys with a relationship and personal interests to manage. She has helped me realize that it's not just about getting through another demanding day; it's about being successful with all I have been blessed with—a family, a career, a lover, a social life, and a personal life of the mind and spirit.

—Laura Fontana, businessperson and mother of two
and client of the author

Bria offers practical and focused advice for today's moms who are trying to do it all: be better wives, raise better children, be better citizens, and be better people. It's possible to strike that balance, and Bria paves a path that's easy for me to follow, regardless of how committed (or overcommitted) I am.

—Dori Culter, businessperson and mother of two

Bria has helped me realize that parenting is just one part of my person. With her help, I have become more in touch with my other capabilities and, as a result, I am a much more complete and happy person.

—Nancy Arcieri, philanthropist and mother of three

Working with Bria has been both supportive and challenging. She can help you push past obstacles that have been holding you back so that you can fully enjoy being the whole you. She really helps you learn how to successfully embrace both motherhood and your individuality. A few small changes can make a world of difference in your life. They did for me!

—Karin Boucher, mother and client of the author

I love Bria's no-nonsense, easy-to-apply approach. Things that seem overwhelming are suddenly simple. I think she's fabulous!

—Janice Levering, businessperson and mother

the balanced mom

raising your kids without losing your self

bria simpson, MA

New Harbinger Publications, Inc.

Publisher's Note

This publication is designed to provide accurate and authoritative information in regard to the subject matter covered. It is sold with the understanding that the publisher is not engaged in rendering psychological, financial, legal, or other professional services. If expert assistance or counseling is needed, the services of a competent professional should be sought.

Distributed in Canada by Raincoast Books

Copyright © 2006 by Bria Simpson
New Harbinger Publications, Inc.
5674 Shattuck Avenue
Oakland, CA 94609
www.newharbinger.com

Cover and text design by Amy Shoup; Acquired by Tesilya Hanauer;
Edited by Brady Kahn

Printed in the United States of America

Library of Congress Cataloging in Publication Data on file
Simpson, Bria.
   The balanced mom : raising your kids without losing your self / Bria Simpson.
      p. cm.
   ISBN-13: 978-1-57224-453-5
   ISBN-10: 1-57224-453-4
 1. Mothers—Psychology. 2. Parenting—Psychological aspects. 3. Mother and child.
4. Self-realization in women. I. Title
   HQ759.S5514 2006
   306.874'3—dc22

15 14 13

10 9 8 7 6 5

The secret of life is balance, and the absence of balance is life's destruction.

—Hazrat Inayat Khan

contents

part 2 the balancing act

part 3 your fabulous family

acknowledgments

i am blessed with many people in my life who have helped me expand myself, balance my own life, and ultimately, find the courage and energy to write this book. I would like to express my gratitude.

First, to my husband Mark (the most balanced dad I know) for being my soul mate for over eighteen years, for your enormous help with this book and with managing our family, and for always supporting my whole self. You are full of life, full of fun, and an extraordinary person to share my life with.

To my children: Cameron, for your sweet demeanor and your excitement throughout my writing process, you helped fuel me every step of the way; MacKenzi, for your remarkable spirit and for making me laugh every day; and Jaden, for being such an endearing and engaging toddler. You are incredibly unique and amazing people. Your faces are always with me and give me such inspiration. I love and adore each of you.

To my parents, Tom and Stephanie Seymour, for showing me that there are no limits to what hard work can achieve, for encouraging me to define my own balance on my own terms, and for teaching me to be proud of my voice. To my father, Andy Bartlett, for showing me the value of living life to its fullest and thinking outside the box. To my mother-in-law, Leigh, for the amazing spirit of life you have shared with us and passed on to my family.

To my sisters, Sara and Anna, for your constant encouragement, your endless enthusiasm, and your honest discussions about my book. To my brother, Bart, for saving my computer, and thus my sanity, on numerous occasions.

I am blessed to do the work I love, and I greatly appreciate my clients for your courage and your openness to new possibilities. To my initial editors, Tesilya Hanauer and Heather Mitchener, for taking the risk with a new author and a new topic. And to the rest of the New Harbinger team, I am grateful for your insights and your support.

To our family friends, the Fandls, the Maltzs, and the Wackermans, with whom we've raised our children, all in search of the proper "balance," for being adventurous with us and for sharing in life's ups and downs. And to all our local friends who help us keep life out here in the burbs fun and interesting. Raising children is a whole lot better when you are surrounded by people you love.

I would not feel complete without thanking our Duke friends and their spouses. You are innovative, remarkable people, you motivate me to be the best I can be, and you were my inspiration for chapter 26, Bring in the Fun!

Finally, I would like to thank my beloved women friends who rallied around me, answered my barrage of questions, helped me develop my thoughts, and shared some of your wisdom for this book: Maria Acebal, Susannah Adelson, Nancy Arcieri, Elaine Bartlett, Carolyn Breslin, Cathy Brienza, Nancy Fandl, Dori Fenenbock, Beth Goddard, Janice Levering, Lynn Maltz, Whitney Nelson, Claudia Remley, Katie Saladucha, Julie Seibold, Merrill Simpson, Carolyn Spahn, Margie Warren, and all of the fabulous women in my book group.

This book is, in large part, a culmination of what I have gained from all of you over the years. Thank you.

introduction

as a life coach who specializes in coaching mothers, and a busy, sometimes crazed mother of three, I've listened to a lot of mommy voices over the years. On the playgrounds, with my clients, with my friends, in current research and the media, at my workshops, and even in myself, I've listened to the voices of discontent. The struggle to be happy, to feel whole, to feel okay about taking care of ourselves as *individuals*—outside of mommyhood. Mothers who wonder, "Why do I feel selfish because I want to work? Or exercise? Or go somewhere, alone?" Mothers who will join a book group or recipe group, but rarely make it on time, or at all, because their children seemingly need them constantly. And mothers who put off their dreams until their children are raised, only to realize, once the kids are gone, that they don't know who they are anymore.

As a group, we've become trapped in micro-mommying, feeling guilty for taking "too much" time for ourselves. The problem is, the minute amount of time you allow for your own development and self-fulfillment has been crammed into the twelve minutes in between car pools every other Wednesday! Many moms have lost touch with the dynamic, capable, amazing women they are. We've perfected modern motherhood with its intense child-focus but have lost pieces of ourselves in the process.

I understand because I've been there myself. I've experienced the same confusion about how to juggle my own needs with the seemingly relentless mommy duties of our generation. And the conclusion I've reached, after much research, work, and observation, is that we need to continue, rather than deny, the development of ourselves to be fulfilled. We need to stop micromanaging our children and let them live their lives and learn their own life lessons. We need to share the load, put our guilt in the graveyard, and rediscover our true passions and interests. We need to take a step back, take a breath, and ensure that our lives reflect our fundamental values.

The term "values" has been thrown around a lot lately. What does it really mean? Our values are our deepest beliefs and convictions about what is really important. That is, if you were to imagine yourself in five years observing your own funeral, what would you hope your family and friends would be saying about you? How would you like to be described as a mother? As an individual? What would you like them to say about what you offered to the world around you? Your answers to these questions reflect your deepest values. If you feel a little out of touch with the answers, you aren't alone. Many of our personal and parenting choices today are driven by the culture we live in, the outside world, rather than by our true values and beliefs, the inside world. This book will help you rediscover your center and allow your life decisions to flow from this authentic place.

There are books that analyze the complexities behind how we have developed our overidentification with the mommy role, but what's lacking is helpful advice about what to do about it. That's what this book provides. It's comprised of little bits of guidance to help center you. My aim is to help you prioritize and learn to say no, to stop caring what those elusive "other people" think, and to make conscious choices based on your own values. I want you to enhance your life by helping you reconnect with your authentic self, your true self, and feel good about it. Ultimately, I want you to discover your happiness and to absolutely love your life.

On your path toward fulfilling yourself, my intention is that you will maintain strong relationships with your children and parent them in ways that promote their own independence, thereby allowing them to grow and giving you the space and security you need to feel good about developing yourself. As you try so fervently to help your children develop into their best selves, I encourage you to refocus some of that energy into living *your* best life. If your children are your greatest priority, as mine are, know that they benefit from seeing you as a whole person. By following the tips in this book, you are not abandoning your children. On the contrary, you are giving them the tools they need to develop fully and value themselves as you continue to develop and value yourself along with them.

I recommend that you begin with the first three chapters, as they are the heart and soul of the book. Beyond that, I encourage you to skip around to explore whatever topic suits your needs at the time. The tips are short and easy to follow, so you can pick up the book at your convenience and immediately put them to use. And keep in mind that what you find helpful now may be different from what you will find helpful a few years from now.

As you work through the book and demonstrate to your children that you matter too, they, in turn, will learn to respect you as a separate individual. By observing you value yourself, they will learn to respect themselves too. And your family will benefit from the joy that can't help but blossom within you, because you are no longer losing your self. You are finding it, nurturing it, and loving it.

I send you my warmest wishes as you discover which tips in this book will help you be *both* a loving mother *and* a dynamic individual. To your well-deserved success and happiness,

Bria

part 1
keep your tank full

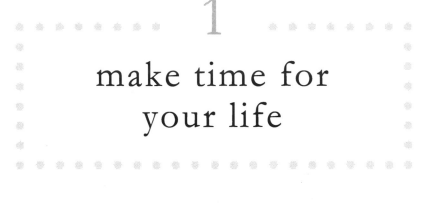

make time for
your life

How we spend our days is, of course, how we spend our lives.

—Annie Dillard

i believe modern moms can "have it all"—just not all at once. A common mistake in our culture is to jump mindlessly from activity to activity. The problem is that we start to feel like we are on autopilot. We become detached from knowing what is most important to us—much less doing what truly matters. Our weekends are no longer a refuge but are a continuation of the stress. Hours turn into days, which turn into months, and our chaotic life starts to pass us by.

It's time to take back your weekends. *It's time to take back your life.* The first step is to make time for it. To better understand where the hours go, write down everything you do for at least four days (two weekdays and the weekend), from the time you wake up to when you go to sleep. Everything. You can enlarge and use the Weekly Schedule Form on page 10 (at the end of this chapter).

Once you've tracked how your life energy is spent for four days, ask yourself some pertinent questions:

- What percentage of your energy is spent on attending to your personal needs, self-care, interests, and real priorities? For many moms, this percentage is quite low, which often leads to burnout, depression, anxiety, or other afflictions.

- What is draining you?

- What can you take out in order to make space for what truly matters?

If you want to create a fulfilling life, you have to make space for what really matters. There's no way around it. To free up some time, consider doing the following:

- **limit your kids' activities.** I suggest you limit the number of organized activities your children are involved in. This may mean each child only participates in one or two activities each week. The number you choose will be influenced by your child's temperament, how many children you have, the time each activity requires, and the total amount of energy you want to devote to these activities. If the other kids at school or on the block are doing three or four activities at a time, reconnect with your deepest values and remind yourself that you and your children need *time and space* to live your best lives. That requires setting limits.

- **limit situations that tend to remain superficial.** Being friendly and cordial is not the same as droning on about superficial stuff. Gossiping and judging others, for example, drains your energy and wastes precious time. Refuse to lower your standards. Limit phone calls and other situations that lend themselves to superficial talk. As you incorporate more of the tips in this book, you also may find that you naturally move away from these situations as you become a more fulfilled, happier individual.

- **learn not to sweat the small stuff.** A slightly messy house or car isn't the end of the world. In my car, you will find empty water bottles or crushed pretzels on any given day. Not something I'm particularly proud of. However, I try to remind myself that allowing some imperfections is necessary to free up energy for more meaningful matters. For more help accepting imperfections, see chapter 5.

- **underschedule yourself.** That's right. Figure out what you can get out of now and keep saying no to more obligations. Become a master mom at saying no. Once you have underscheduled yourself and live in alignment with your highest priorities, you can gradually add more activities if you have the space for them. As you underschedule and prioritize better, you will enjoy the almighty sense of *balance*, because you have learned not to bring in more until you've let something else go.

You do have control over how your life takes shape. It may not be easy to delete some activities from your life and let go of the small stuff. But, if you really want to enhance your life, you must make space for your priorities. It's that simple.

weekly schedule form

	Monday	Tuesday	Wednesday	Thursday	Friday	Saturday	Sunday
6:00A.M.	MOLLY AWAKE	MOLLY AWAKE				MOLLY AWAKE	
7:00A.M.		TO SCHOOL	TO SCHOOL	TO SCHOOL	7A MTG		
8:00A.M.		MOM WORKS	WORK	WORK	MTG		
9:00A.M.	MOLLY SCHOOL				" FREE		
10:00A.M.						GYMNAST ICS	SWIM
11:00A.M.	MOM WORKS						
12:00P.M.					WORK	MOLLY	NAP
1:00P.M.							
2:00P.M.							
3:00P.M.							
4:00P.M.							
5:00P.M.							
6:00P.M.	GET MOLLY	GET MOLLY					
7:00P.M.	MAKE DINNER	"	"	"	"		
8:00P.M.	MOLLY BATH	"	"	"	"		
9:00P.M.	MOLLY BED	"	"	"	"		
10:00P.M.	FREE TIME	"	"	"	"		

SLEEP ? WORK

2

live your values

Wisdom may be defined as knowing what is important and what isn't important. In wisdom we see the whole picture.

—John Bradshaw

We are so bombarded with choices, it can be a real challenge to choose what to bring into our lives and what to leave out. To help you try to make the best choices for you and your family, connect with your deepest values, your core convictions about what really matters. When your decisions are led by your values, rather than by what other parents are doing or saying, you are living authentically, in alignment with your true self. You feel confident and energized by your choices because they reflect *the real you*.

Consider using this chapter as a writing exercise to help you identify with and integrate your deepest values. Write your answers in your journal or use the worksheet at the end of this chapter.

- **what qualities do you most respect in yourself and in others? how do your choices and behaviors exemplify these characteristics?** Do you admire creativity? Spirituality? Generosity toward others in need? Individuality? Self-confidence? Having fun? What rings true for you, and how can you set aside some time to enhance these qualities in your life?

- **what are some of your fondest memories as a child and what values do they reflect? how can these values be reflected in your adult life?** Some of my favorite memories, for instance, are of traveling to other countries and learning about different cultures and beliefs. These experiences have helped me be more open-minded, a trait I highly value. My intention is to continue to travel with my children to a variety of countries and to find other ways to obtain new perspectives. Perhaps you have fond memories about family get-togethers and you value family traditions. Or, maybe thinking about the times you read books brings a smile to your face. In this instance, you may value solitary time. Write down some of your fondest memories, what values they reflect, and how these values can be woven into your adult life.

- **imagine yourself at the end of your life.** What do you hope your life has included by the time you die? If you were to die tomorrow, what would you have missed out on? When many people do this exercise, they realize they need to spend more time taking care of themselves and doing what they really enjoy. They need to take more risks and really live life to its fullest. Use this exercise as a wake-up call to clarify your values and priorities.

- **what do you really want your children to remember about their childhoods?** Close your eyes and visualize the answers. What are all the pieces that are important? Think about life experiences and life lessons: time with parents, with siblings, with friends; playing sports; exploring/discovering; learning music; spiritual lessons; giving to others; and so on. Write down ways to make those memories happen.

- **how do you want your children to remember you?** Busy, chaotic, and chronically tired—with a clean and tidy house? Or relatively calm, happy, and fulfilled—with a slightly messy house? Do you want them to remember you yelling so that they could move faster and fit in more activities, or do you want them to remember you sitting contentedly with them as they played or finished their homework? Do you want them to remember you solely as their caretaker, or do you want them to remember you having your own interests and passions? Your answers reflect your true values.

- if you want to develop and maintain close relationships with your children, how do your behaviors encourage this? Do you play or spend time with them in ways that you both enjoy? Do you set aside time when you are fully present with your children?

- if you have a spouse, how do your behaviors reflect your desire for a mutually beneficial and enjoyable relationship? Do you make regular, quality time to talk with your spouse or partner? Do you date each other to keep the communication open and the romance alive? What type of marital interactions do your children typically observe?

It's important to recognize what really matters to your authentic self. You've got one shot at this lifetime. Ideally, your values, for yourself and for your family, are reflected in how you spend your time. Make the time to observe how you use your energy, reconnect with your highest values, and make some changes to better align your behaviors with these values. You'll be glad you did!

values worksheet

1. What qualities do you most respect in yourself and in others?

   Integrity, hardworking, genuine, calm

2. What are some ways you can enhance these qualities in your life?

   avoid taking work home (?)

3. What are some of your fondest memories as a child, and what values do they reflect?

   freedom, being around friends, outdoors vs watching TV. social!

   How can some of these values be reflected in your adult life?

   personal time, time with friends, time with hubby

   How can they be reflected in your children's lives?

   Cultivating neighborhood environment that she gets together with others, stressing outdoors

15

4. What do you really want your children to remember about their childhoods?

> beauty of Oregon, friends/get togethers in neighborhood, eating healthy, family time

5. If you want to develop and maintain close relationships with your children, how do your behaviors encourage this?

> work at work, home @ home, family activities

6. Do you value having a strong, mutually beneficial, and enjoyable relationship with your spouse/partner? If so, how do your behaviors consistently reflect this value?

> Yes! We do monthly date time. I'd love to get evenings back

3

get your priorities straight

The first step to getting the things you want out of life is this: Decide what you want.

—Ben Stein

now that you've cleared out some space in your life and reconnected with your core values, it's time to ensure that how you spend your energy reflects these values. Read on for some tips to help you define your highest priorities and bring them into your life.

- **as you focus on your need for balance and a whole life, write down your highest priorities.** You may want to include excellent self-care, your marriage/partnership, your children, spirituality, social support, having fun, personal growth, and interests and passions. If paid work is a priority, include that as well. Write down specific goals for fulfillment in each area. For instance, under self-care, you might want to write "yoga, meditation, monthly massages, regular exercise," and so on. You can use the highest-priorities list at the end of this chapter.

- **make sure your values are reflected in your highest priorities.** Review your values worksheet (see chapter 2) and incorporate these values into your highest-priorities list. If you want to teach your children to serve others, for instance, you might want to carve out some time to work together in a soup kitchen or participate as a family in a charity walk or bike ride. As you read further in this book, you may get some new ideas, as well.

- **after you have freed up some time in your schedule by taking out some lower priorities, figure out how to bring in pieces from each of your highest priorities.** Create a new weekly schedule. Don't settle for anything less than taking good care of yourself, incorporating fulfilling activities, spending quality time with your children and partner, and living a balanced life.

- **once you've begun underscheduling yourself (see chapter 1), you may find that you need to practice the art of saying no even more, to make time for what really matters.** The next time you are asked to add something into your life, review your highest-priorities list. If it's not on that list, just say no. For instance, many moms with young children, myself included, have learned that now is the time to donate money to charities, and later is the opportunity to donate time. If you need some social support, call on those true friends who encourage your whole self.

- **post your list to constantly remind yourself of your real priorities.** Many people benefit from visualizing life lessons they want to remember on a daily basis. Consider posting your highest-priorities list in a specific area, such as on the bathroom mirror or by the phone, to help you stay on track.

It takes conscious thought and discipline to create a balanced life that is firmly grounded in your values and highest priorities. But it can be done. Be wise with how you spend your precious time and energy, and you will be on track for a rewarding life.

highest-priorities list

Spend some time brainstorming and then write how you would ideally spend your time in the following areas. You want to be realistic
yet also creative. Don't be afraid to think outside the box and do
things differently. This list should reflect your unique self, so complete it however makes the most sense to you.

It's wise to continually check in with yourself and update your
highest priorities. When you are finished, make sure that most of
your priorities are included in your weekly schedule. Schedule some
of your bigger endeavors, like charitable works, into your annual
calendar.

self-care:

monthly massage(?)
10 min to myself daily - meditating,
                    reading? being
                          creative

personal growth:

- exploring travel, global work as a mom
- exploring meditation.

paid or volunteer work:

work less at same income with opportunity to move forward when Molly is older.

children's personal growth:

Continue varied activities → sports, language, arts, playdates, community service

quality time with spouse or partner:

weekly to bimonthly dates with Jeff!

quality time with children/family:

6-9pm each day is family time ☺ (during wk)
Sunday hikes during summer (or wknd family activity aside from organized activity each Sat/Sun

spiritual development:

not sure

interests and passions:

travel, cooking, making our home look better

social support:

- more great babysitters other than CoCo
- cultivating more LO friendships
- keeping in touch with other Parkland friends

having fun:

trips away, trying new restaurants

other priorities:

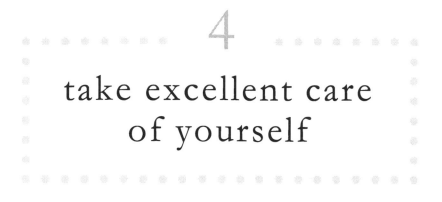

take excellent care
of yourself

I know for sure that you can't give what you don't have. If you allow yourself to be depleted to the point where your emotional and spiritual tank is empty and you're running on fumes out of habit, everyone loses. Especially you.

—Oprah

With all of the pressures of modern motherhood and the challenges to living a peaceful, balanced life, it's easy to neglect yourself. But you truly can't take care of others if you aren't taking good care of yourself. Your body has a way of telling you that you are ignoring yourself and burning out, as you experience exhaustion, depression, anxiety, physical ailments, insomnia, or alcohol dependency.

Do what you can to prevent these signs of burnout. Ask yourself, "How full is my tank?" Picture a scale from 1 to 10 on which 1 is feeling consumed by signs of burnout and 10 is feeling joyful, balanced, and peaceful. Your goal is to stay between a 7 and a 10. Where are you today? Check in with yourself on a regular basis and incorporate the necessary changes to keep your tank filled.

Here are some ways to do it:

- **manage your stress.** Research demonstrates that an inability to manage stress can impair your emotional, mental, and physical health. Connecting with your highest values and priorities, becoming comfortable with saying no, and insisting on having some time to yourself will all help with maintaining your health. Numerous tips in this book will help you manage your stress. Use them!

- **exercise regularly and enjoy it!** Regular moderate exercise has been shown to decrease stress, insomnia, anxiety, and depression. Research shows that thirty to forty-five minutes of cardiovascular exercise is the optimal amount of time to improve your mood. This is one tip you can't afford to ignore! Get creative so you can exercise at least four times a week and keep it fun. Consider taking different aerobic and yoga classes, meeting a friend, hiring a trainer, or exercising outdoors and enjoying the sunshine.

- **eat well.** You've heard this one before. Good nutrition is another essential that affects your well-being in a multitude of ways—improving your energy levels, sense of well-being, and long-term health. If you don't know how to eat well, read some of the updated nutrition books. And then start doing it!

- **get enough sleep.** This sounds simple but is often overlooked. Important neurotransmitters and hormones are only produced sufficiently when you get adequate sleep. Most of us need at least eight hours of sleep at night. Many of us also benefit from a brief nap some afternoons (I know I do!). We can learn from the lovely European tradition of closing up shop and taking siestas after lunch. Listen to your body and get as much sleep as you need to feel well-rested each day.

- **create a sacred space for your time alone.** Carve out a space for yourself, such as a private room or a screened-off area. Keep it free of clutter and fill it with whatever soothes you, perhaps candles, pictures, or plants. Make sure everyone understands that you are not to be interrupted when you are in your sacred space. Post a homemade "Mother Goddess Needs Privacy" sign on the outside. Your sacred space is for your solitary, slowed-down time. Use it to be creative, listen to classical music, write in a journal, meditate, stand on your head ... or whatever else you feel like doing alone.

This chapter covered some of the basics for a solid foundation of self-care. Following other tips in this book will also contribute to your overall well-being. Remember, when you attend to your own needs and keep your tank full, you are happier, more energized, and much more able to reach out to others.

5

ditch mommy perfection

The thing that is really hard, and really amazing, is giving up on being perfect and beginning the work on being yourself.

—Anna Quindlen

mommy perfection has become an image of a well-dressed woman who organizes and manages every detail of her overscheduled family, keeps a perfectly tidy home, and, absolutely without fail, actively supports her children's every endeavor. She may possibly cram in an area of personal interest—if and only if it doesn't interfere with all the previous, much more important duties. This vision of the perfect mommy has become all too common. And all too impossible to achieve.

Somewhere along the line, we allowed this impossible image of perfect motherhood to evolve. In the process, endless mothers chronically feel like they aren't good enough, because they are unable to attain the unattainable.

Thankfully, we can recognize the madness and let it go. When you create a fulfilling and balanced life for yourself, you stop desiring perfection. As your self-image becomes less influenced by what others think, and more driven by your inner voice, you can begin to live authentically. You are liberated to be yourself. In doing so, you don't care as much that you forgot to put on mascara, or that your kid's clothes are on inside out, or that your house is a little cluttered at times.

Consider these suggestions to help you let go of mommy perfectionism and replace it with a healthy, life-affirming perspective of motherhood:

- **realize that perfectionism limits your growth.** Living your best life doesn't include trying to be perfect. On the contrary, when you try to achieve the impossible, you set yourself up for failure. You can't feel good about yourself when you constantly feel that you aren't measuring up. Recognize the constraints of perfectionism, and let it go.

- **consciously allow for imperfections.** Accept that you won't always look your best. Allow that you will sometimes be late. As long as you have kids in your home, resist the urge to demand an immaculate house at all times. Let some imperfections become a regular part of your life. In doing so, you are freeing yourself to be human.

- **engage in enriching endeavors.** Make sure that some of your energy is focused on hobbies, work, and/or activities that are meaningful and rewarding to you. It's much easier to let go of perfectionism when you have some enriching outlets that require your attention.

- **embrace all of your different roles.** Putting all of your eggs in one basket—be it motherhood, work, or anything else—severely limits you and puts you at risk for perfectionism and burning out. Make time for all your roles, such as individual, wife, sister, mother, and friend. Regularly take excellent care of yourself. Balance your life. Get some good ideas from this book and put them to use!

- **recognize that the perfect mommy image is harmful.** Don't be a part of the problem, be a part of the solution. Refrain from comments that may contribute to mommy perfectionism, such as "how *do* you do it all?" or "you are always so perfectly dressed and put together." Replace your thoughts and comments about being "perfect" with encouragement for a healthy balance instead.

The perfect mommy image is damaging to us all. Let's agree to ditch it. Take excellent care of yourself, keep a healthy balance, put your energy into meaningful pursuits … and notice how you just don't care as much anymore about being perfect!

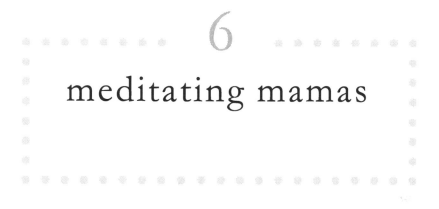

6

meditating mamas

To maintain sanity in such an era, we may have to become intimate with stillness ... if it is healing for us when faced with life-threatening and chronic diseases, how can it not be healing for us in the face of the dis-ease of feeling totally and chronically overwhelmed ...

—Jon Kabat-Zinn

If you want to enjoy your daily life, it is exceptionally helpful to slow down for part of the day and focus on your breath. Research has shown that periods of meditation—of focusing on your breath—helps us transcend worries, lower anxiety, diminish depression, and increase clarity. Meditation balances our moods and enhances our ability to connect fully with who we are.

Does this sound hokey? I understand if it does. It did for me before I added meditation and yoga into my life. I thought that people who sat around just to breathe must be seriously lacking stimulation in their lives. Now I revel in the benefits and hope that you will, as well.

When you meditate, at first, you may not notice much. You may be telling yourself, "Aha! I was right. Only really weird people meditate. I'm not getting anything out of this because I am simply *not* that weird." You may try so hard to "get it right" that you are missing the point—to relax and be in the moment. In our Western culture, we are programmed to believe that without "doing," we are wasting our time. Nothing could be further from the truth.

The benefits of meditation are powerful. It becomes easier to let go of judgment. You start to feel better and the small stuff begins to appear just as it really is—small. You can actually remember the end of a sentence you just started! You are centered.

Friends may even start to ask you how you handle all the stresses in life so well. One day you wake up and think, "Wow, I am actually a calmer person." If you come from a life in overdrive, as I have, that is a *real* accomplishment.

The primary objective of meditation is to focus on your breath. The thoughts are still there—dinner still has to be made or bought and that person who was rude to you may still annoy you. Just let the thoughts wash over you and come back to your breath.

A few tips on becoming a meditating mama:

- **find a quiet place to meditate.** Unplug your phone, and make sure you won't be interrupted by anyone. Consider using your sacred space (see chapter 4).

- **sit in a comfortable, upright position, cross-legged, or lie flat on your back on the floor.** Try each position at different times and pick what suits you best.

- **close your eyes, take three or four deep breaths, and then start to breathe gently.** Let your thoughts drift away and focus on your breath.

- **as your thoughts jump around, come back to your breath.**

- **start with five minutes and try to build up to at least fifteen minutes, at least three times a week.** Meditating gets easier with practice.

- **it's okay if you fall asleep.** Mr. Kabat-Zinn, a guru on the subject, believes that you will sleep more peacefully if you meditate first. If you are prone to sleep when you meditate, set a gentle-music type of alarm clock if you need to wake up at a certain time.

- **create a regular time in your schedule to meditate.** Generally, first thing in the morning, during children's naptime, or before bed works best. Schedule it and commit to meditating at least three times a week.

- **consider writing in a journal for a few minutes after you meditate.** You may come out of meditation with more clarity. Sometimes it's helpful to jot down your thoughts. They are often meaningful and may help guide you in some way.

That's it! It's really not hard and it's actually not all that weird. If you are still resistant, or you just prefer a more physical approach to relaxation and connection with your inner self, start with yoga (see chapter 16). Yoga has many of the same benefits and often incorporates periods of meditation. Open your mind and remember, you don't have to tell a soul!

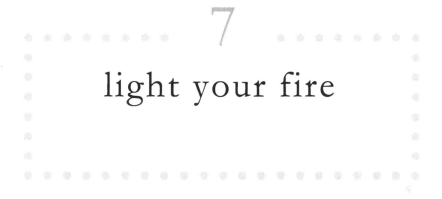

7

light your fire

*Find the passion. It takes great passion and great energy
to do anything creative. I would go so far as to say that you
can't do it without that passion.*

—Agnes de Mille

We all have fires in our hearts—true passions. Amazingly, when we identify and integrate some passionate interests into our lives, we elevate ourselves. We enjoy more energy, a more optimistic outlook, and a greater ability to let go of nonsense and nonessentials. Exploring your authentic passions can go a long way toward honoring your unique self as you raise your children.

To help you discover and incorporate your passions, consider the following:

- **identify your authentic passions.** While engaged in a true passion, time often passes without your awareness. You are in the flow of something you love, and it's easy to get lost in the present moment. What activities make you feel this way?

- **the core of your passions can often be found in your childhood.** Remind yourself what you loved to do as a child. How can similar experiences be included in your adult life? For instance, I used to write poems for my first grade teacher every week—just for the fun of it. I recently became reacquainted with my passion for writing when I decided to start my online newsletter and write this book.

- **make a list of your true passions.** In a journal, list three to five things that you love to do. How can you bring some of these things into your life?

- **schedule time to commit to your passions.** Without making the time, you can't bring your passions to life. You may need to call on some of the organizational and scheduling skills reviewed in this book to help make your passions a priority.

- **join a group whose members have similar interests.** Many moms discover that joining a group whose members have similar interests promotes greater connections among women than a "mommy" group does alone. If all you have in common with other group members is that you've all reproduced, it may not be stimulating enough. Consider hobbies you enjoy—gardening, writing, running, yoga, computers, artistic creations, politics, and so on. Scour the Internet, local papers, and community boards, and you are likely to find a group of women who share similar interests. If you can't find one, start one!

- **the expression of your passions may change over time.** A passion at age fifteen may be expressed differently at age fifty. For instance, a soccer fanatic as a teenager may become a soccer coach in later years. If you allow yourself, you will continue to grow and express yourself throughout your lifetime.

- **if you still have difficulty discovering your passions or integrating them into your life, consider hiring a life coach.** What you may need is a combination of the right questions to excavate your passions and the support and encouragement to bring them to life.

A joyful life requires saving time and energy for activities that you avidly enjoy. Life is too short not to enjoy it to the fullest. What passions will you bring into your life this week?

8

caviar complaints

To be satisfied with what one has; that is wealth.

—Mark Twain

if you live with free choice and have the financial means to cover basic necessities, consider yourself extremely fortunate. Even your ability to read this book is a gift. Much of the world does not share such basic freedoms.

Unfortunately, it's easy to lose perspective and get bogged down in what are really problems of the fortunate, what I call "caviar complaints." You lose sleep because your son didn't make the "right" basketball team. You obsess about the inevitable imperfections of your body or your house. You worry because not every person likes you. These are problems you worry about *because you can*. If your basic survival were at stake, you wouldn't worry about these caviar complaints.

But even though you can worry about caviar complaints, you really don't want to. It's wasted energy. Shift your thinking to maintain a healthy perspective. Here's how:

- **deal directly with the big stuff and let the rest go.**
  One way to thrive in this overactive culture is to learn what to put your attention on and what to ignore. The big stuff— such as taking good care of yourself, saving more than you spend, discovering your passions, living your values—deserves your time and energy. The little issues—such as keeping up with the gossip on the playground or at the watercooler at work—do not.

- **ask yourself, will this matter a year from now?**
  This is an excellent question to help you separate the big stuff from the small stuff. Too much paperwork or this morning's traffic jam won't matter in a year. Ignoring a chronic, gnawing feeling of emptiness and boredom may well haunt you a year from now. Focus on the big stuff and let the rest go.

- **practice gratitude daily and keep your life whole.**
  Use the tips in this book to appreciate what you have and ensure that your life is rewarding—not only as a mom but as an individual as well. When you feel fulfilled and in balance, it's much easier to rise above the small stuff.

Work through the big problems in life. Free yourself from caviar complaints and open yourself up for a life of abundance.

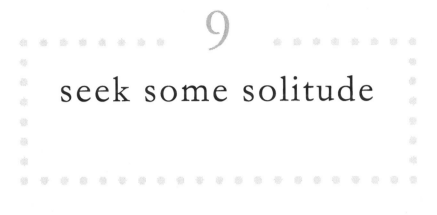

9

seek some solitude

Before you can get real, you've got to get quiet.

—Suzanne Zoglio

d o you find that your life is filled with constant chatter? Your day has about nine hundred wakeful minutes. How many of those are spent in quiet solitude? Do you turn on the television just for background noise? What about the radio in the car … is it always on? The iPod when you exercise? The cell phone when you don't? Our lives have reached a frenetic pace, with too much noise. How can we think clearly or know ourselves if we are in a state of continuous chatter?

If you want to live your life to the fullest, you need time to be alone. You need space to rest your brain. You need some quiet to allow your authentic self to emerge.

Consider these suggestions to help you create the space and quiet you need:

- **do some activities alone.** When many of my clients begin working with me, they realize how little time they spend alone. As they start spending more time in solitude, most are quick to recognize how much they love it. When you ride a bike, shop, or catch a movie, alone, you get to do what *you* want, without trying to meet the needs or desires of others. For most modern mamas, this precious time is rare. If you are always with children or other people, start doing more activities by yourself and notice how you feel.

- **find an individual hobby that engages you.** Think about what you truly love to do. Garden? Spend time in nature? Write? Read? Paint? Let your mind drift off, thinking about what you like to do. Where does it take you?

- **get up before your family.** Go to bed earlier, so you can get up earlier. Revel in the unbelievable quiet. Read the paper, meditate, write in your journal, enjoy a quiet cup of coffee. Get outside when you can. Start your day in peaceful solitude and notice how much better your day begins.

- **unplug at home or work.** Make sure you have at least brief periods of time in your day when you aren't answering the phone, the door, your e-mail, and attending to others. Take at least half of your daily mommy time-outs (see chapter 25) in quiet solitude. Go outside for a walk. Eat lunch alone. Focus on what you are doing and let the rest go.

- **unplug in the car.** When you find yourself driving alone, experience silence for at least some of the time. Resist the urge to play music or chatter on the cell phone for the entire time. Perhaps it's time to listen to issues inside your head that need to be worked out. Or maybe it's time just to be mindful of the present moment and let your brain unwind.

- **find your spiritual self.** Spend time alone in whatever setting helps you connect with your soul or a higher power. This may mean attending a public place of worship, spending time alone in nature, meditating, or doing whatever suits your spiritual self. Discover what it is for you. For most of us, this connection is felt most deeply if we are either physically alone or in periods of quiet.

- **teach yourself and your children that it is okay to be alone.** When I have gone on solitary retreats, I've noticed that I have to force myself to go out to eat alone. It feels strange. But if I just do it, I find that I enjoy it. Remind yourself that it takes courage to be different and that, in our culture, being alone sometimes feels different. Don't let that stop you. Set an example for your children and teach them that spending some time alone is really a source of strength.

If we never stop the noise, we don't hear ourselves. If we're always with others, we don't know ourselves. Separate some. Make time for quiet and solitude. And enjoy what emerges—the real you.

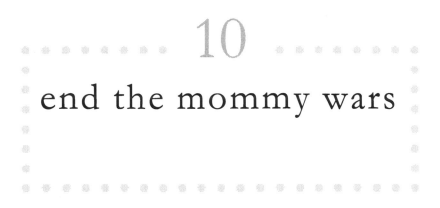

10

end the mommy wars

A man has to be Attila the Hun to be called ruthless.
All a woman has to do is put you on hold.

—Marlo Thomas

as moms, we can be our own worst enemies. When we judge others, and especially when we talk about it, we are degrading ourselves. Contrary to what we may think, we really don't know what's best for other people. We each have unique life experiences, genetics, and temperaments that shape who we are. Whether working outside the home—part-time, full-time, or not at all—is ideal, for example, can only be determined by the woman in the driver's seat.

In the same vein, children are unique. How to best parent a child differs across families and across children. In my own family, my older daughter and my son are incredibly different. Among my son's greatest strengths are his compassion and his analytical mind. My daughter's greatest strengths include her assertiveness and her spirit. Because of their differences in temperament and personality, I've learned that they benefit from some differences in parenting styles. It's not something that a parenting book or another parent can necessarily teach, but it's something I've learned from tuning into my intuition.

In essence, there is no one size fits all when it comes to how to be a good mom or how to balance it all. What's important is to focus on your inner voice, work on living your best life, and let others live theirs. Consider these suggestions:

- **don't shrink yourself to make others feel more comfortable.** Whatever path you choose, especially when it requires courage, accept that some people may respond negatively. Understand that people tend to react the strongest when others have touched something that they are conflicted with inside themselves. When others judge you, it's really about themselves. Keep yourself separate and don't allow yourself to get wrapped up in other people's issues.

- **your parenting choices may disappoint others.** Accept this fact of life. As a mom, it's your job to do the best you can with your parenting choices. There will always be people who think you are a negligent mom if you aren't at every school pickup or if you consistently take time for yourself. Who cares? Remind yourself that their disapproval has everything to do with their own issues and very little to do with you. Ignore the judgments and stay focused on your own values and inner guidance.

- **until you walk in her shoes, and you never will, don't judge.** What works for you won't work for everyone. Open your heart and mind and recognize that we are all struggling to do the best we can. We each have a unique journey. In fact, with respect to your own development and with your parenting decisions, choices you make now may be very different from choices you will make later. We are at our best when we allow ourselves, and others, to grow and change over time. It's your aspiration to live your best life. Let others figure out how to live theirs.

- **rise above and live your glorious life.** It's much easier to rise above the gossip and pessimism if you have a fulfilling, whole life of your own. Many of the tips in this book will help you focus on your priorities and what really matters, allowing you to stop wasting energy on negativity.

Let's end the mommy wars. By honoring other moms' choices and focusing on our own growth and life balance, we can transcend judgment and enjoy some mommy peace.

11

count your blessings

Gratitude unlocks the fullness of life ... It turns denial into acceptance, chaos to order, confusion to clarity ... Gratitude makes sense of our past, brings peace for today, and creates a vision for tomorrow.

—Melody Beattie

Without gratitude, it's easy to let negative thoughts invade your life. Recognizing and feeling grateful forces you to focus on what *is* working in your life. Rooted in such a place, you flourish. Consider the following:

- **create a family ritual around gratitude.** Children can easily experience the benefits of gratitude if they are asked to consider it regularly. A simple blessing before dinner, such as "Thank you for our food and for the love in our family and in the world," helps kids feel grateful. You can also include something each of you appreciates about your day, yourselves, or each other.

- **create a personal ritual around gratitude.** Consider expressing your gratitude in a journal. Your thoughts can be about simple occurrences, such as your appreciation for quiet time or a sunny day, or about greater blessings in your life, such as your joy for the connection you feel with your children or spouse. Another idea is to write your thoughts of gratitude on sticky notes and place them in areas you will observe daily. Or, perhaps you would prefer to use the power of prayer which is inherent in many religions. Discover what works best for you.

- **practice your rituals at specific times several times a week.** A behavior is more likely to continue if there is a designated time frame and pattern attached to it. Some people prefer rituals of gratitude first thing in the morning; others prefer them at the end of the day. Whatever you choose, observe how your days start off better or your sleep becomes more peaceful.

When you are conscious of your blessings, you are grounded in joy, strength, and a sense of fulfillment. There is a spiritual law that states that the more you have and are grateful for, the more you will receive. In essence, more is given to you *because* you are grateful for what you have. Regularly practice gratitude, watch your sense of abundance grow, and enjoy the transformation!

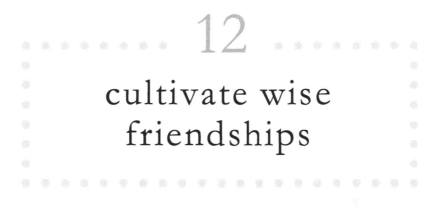

12

cultivate wise friendships

Be who you are and say what you feel, because those who mind don't matter and those who matter don't mind.

—Dr. Seuss

Wise friendships are the ones that support and accept your authentic, real self. Good friends are the ones you really feel comfortable being yourself around. Your experiences with friends can really lift you up, support you, and encourage you to live your best life ... *if* you choose the right people. Do yourself a favor. Enrich your life by cultivating wise friendships.

Consider these suggestions:

- increase time with women who really lift you up.
  If your friendship is really based on mutual fondness and
  respect for each other, you generally feel more energized after
  spending time with that person. Perhaps you feel exuberant
  because you shared some great ideas with each other. Maybe
  she was able to support the latest passion you've brought into
  your life. Or perhaps she just listened well on a topic you
  needed to share. When you find friends who lift you higher,
  it's wise to keep them in your life. And be sure you give back
  to them as well.

- spend less time with those who bring you down.
  If you consistently feel more anxious, more depressed, or
  more drained after sharing time with someone, this is not a
  meaningful friendship for you. It's probably not for her
  either. Don't sweat it. But do remember that your time and
  energy are valuable. By minimizing your time with people
  who bring you lower, you free yourself for more enriching
  people and experiences.

- participate in groups that appeal to you. Don't
  waste your time in groups that you don't enjoy or feel comfortable in. Some groups may lack people who genuinely
  interest you. So don't go. It's far better to spend your energy
  searching for, or even creating, social or interest groups that
  you find stimulating.

- **trust your instincts.** It's amazing how much time we'll put into analyzing why a particular group or friendship doesn't seem good for us. Save your energy. Trust your gut with people and your life will become more satisfying.

Your life is short. As a mom and a dynamic individual, you have a limited amount of social time. Spend it wisely.

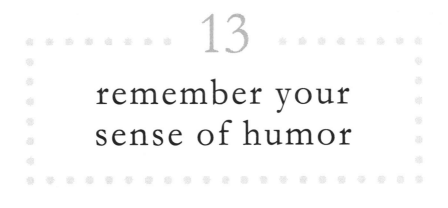

13

remember your
sense of humor

*Blessed are they who laugh at themselves, for
they will never cease to be amused!*

—Anonymous

have you ever noticed that most people who make you laugh, or who laugh at themselves, are pleasant to hang out with? They make life seem lighter ... more fun ... more enjoyable.

If you've lost your sense of humor, it's time to find it. Lighten up. Find the humor. I promise it's there.

Consider these tips to get you started:

- **show me the funny!** Laughing is good for your immune system and raises your spirits. Rent funny movies, see a comedian, go out with people who make you laugh. Keep the healing power of laughter in the forefront of your mind.

- **find your funny self.** You *are* a funny person, in some way, shape, or form. Is it your wit? Your silly jokes? The way you tell stories? Your latest dance moves? Find it, own it, express it!

- **rather than stress, laugh!** Research documents that stress is closely related to serious illnesses. Stress affects all aspects of life. One way to lessen stress is to shift your perspective: You can't tell the difference between weeds in your yard and the real plants? The toilet won't flush, again? You arrive at work with the price tag on the back of your shirt? Oh well … shake it off with a smile. Finding the humor in small annoyances can be just the ticket to a more easygoing life.

- **let go of some of your children's problems and smile instead.** Sometimes you just need to laugh when your two-year-old paints herself with margarine (as mine did) or your ten-year-old left his homework at home—again! Problems with children are inevitable. Just give a consequence, if a consequence is warranted, and then let the issue go with a smile.

- **encourage your children's sense of humor.** Some kids are funny by nature; others just seem born to take life seriously. If you've got one of the latter, help him lighten up. Laugh at her jokes (as painful as this might be). Teach him how to be silly with you—skip instead of walk, imitate the goofballs on television ... Show her how to laugh at some of life's problems. Helping your children get in touch with their humor, their lighter side, may be one of the greatest gifts you give them.

Don't underestimate the power of a fabulous sense of humor. Sometimes lightening up is just what is needed to enjoy motherhood and life. Remind your kids, and yourself, not to take life too seriously. And then make sure you laugh every day.

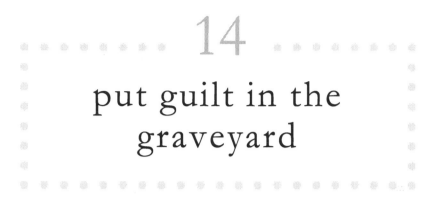

14

put guilt in the graveyard

Show me a woman who doesn't feel guilt and I'll show you a man.

—Erica Jong

absolutely no one can make you feel guilty, unless you let them. But a lot of us feel guilty a lot of the time. Modern moms feel guilty if we aren't at every school pickup or don't attend all of the endless birthday parties or can't cheer on every sporting event for all of our children. But if you live your life trying to uphold modern mommy madness, it's difficult to be happy. Because you can't do everything and still be good to yourself. So stop trying.

The reality is, you can't take good care of others until you stand strong on your own two feet. That requires taking excellent care of yourself, asking for help when you need it, saying no to what is not on your highest-priorities list, and remaining committed to living your best life. As you work through this book and take the pieces that you need to create a more balanced, fulfilling life, rise above the guilt.

Here are some tips to help you along the way:

- **if you feel guilty for taking time for yourself, remind yourself of all that you do for others.** Review your weekly schedule and recognize how much you do to run your household and care for your family. Most mothers are startled when they consciously add up the energy they put into caring for everyone else.

- **recognize that you can't be strong for others until you are a source of strength for yourself.** When your tank is empty, you aren't giving much to others. Your energy is low and you feel scattered. When your tank is full, however, you are joyous and have much more to share with the world around you.

- **stop the endless mommy guilt.** When you spend quality time with your children every week, listen consistently, and interact regularly with your family, you are giving your children what they need. They are priorities in your life, but they don't define you. They need to understand that you have a life outside of them. Let them know that you will do your best to attend their functions and be an integral part of their life but that you have personal needs, as well, that must be respected.

- **support other moms in their decisions.** One way we can stop the mommy madness of our generation is to support each other in our decisions to be strong women. When you notice a mom pursue an interest or develop herself in some way, congratulate her! Help shift the focus from all mom to whole person.

- **if you find yourself too swayed by the opinions of others, reconnect with your highest-priorities list (see chapter 3).** Your true priorities reflect your most authentic desires. Use your inner self to guide you, not the judgments of others. Your real friends will respect your priorities, even if they don't understand them.

You are too wise to let yourself feel guilty for taking good care of yourself and developing as a whole person. Stand strong with your priorities and values, and put guilt where it belongs—in the graveyard.

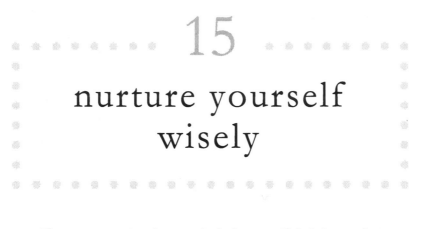

15

nurture yourself
wisely

If your compassion does not include yourself, it is incomplete.

—the Buddha

ave you ever noticed that mothers tend to be reluctant to really love and care for *themselves*? It's time to move past this resistance. Nurture yourself, and your children will learn that not only do you care for them, but you also care about yourself. By valuing yourself, you are encouraging them to love and value themselves. Is there a greater gift you can give to them ... or to yourself?

- **focus on your hottest attributes.** Write down five traits that you love about yourself. Remind yourself daily of your strengths. A healthy self-esteem makes it a lot easier to live your best life—and ignore what isn't important.

- **get a regular massage or reflexology treatment.** Massage and reflexology have been shown to relieve stress, increase energy, decrease depression, help regulate hormones, and improve overall health. These treatments are well worth getting into the budget. When writing this book, I committed to getting weekly Chinese massages, and they greatly enhanced my energy and feelings of well-being throughout the process. Why not enjoy these benefits as a regular part of life?

- **minimize distractions.** How did we get to the point where we cut people off in a phone conversation to take another call that we can't really take because we're already talking to someone else? Get rid of "call waiting," and let those messages go to voice mail when you are on the phone. Let the answering machine pick up your phone calls when you are busy. Try to focus on individual tasks, such as paying bills, without running back and forth to other activities at the same time. Your brain needs a break from constant chaos. Minimizing distractions is essential for a peaceful life.

- **make time for solitude.** It is in the stillness that you get to know yourself and your soul. The universe works in mysterious ways when you quiet your mind and listen.

- **write in a journal.** Writing down your thoughts and feelings helps you connect to your deepest, most authentic self.

It also helps you air frustrations, so you don't continue to clutter your mind with negativity. Make journal writing a routine, and notice how you start to feel more in touch with yourself.

- **schedule in a hobby that slows you down.** Consider writing, gentle yoga, gardening, painting, or something else that takes you out of the rat race and into slower motion.

- **get in tune with your body.** Some people have more energy in the mornings and others are more energized in late afternoons. Research demonstrates that at least a few days before menstruation, you physically need more rest and less action. Instead of fighting your fatigue or mood swings, listen to them. Organize your productivity around your highest energy cycles, take it down a notch during premenstrual times, and enjoy the well-being that arises when you are in tune with your body.

- **take family vacations.** Your vacation may be a cultural trip to another country, some lazy days at the beach, or camping in the woods. The point is to take time off from your busy lives to live in the present and enjoy each other outside of your daily routines.

- **take some mini-retreats alone.** Try to take a few days alone somewhere. This has done wonders for mothers I know who returned refreshed, rejuvenated, and ready to take on their daily duties with strength. At the very least, manage to take a night off alone at a local hotel, sleep in, and rest your soul.

- **give yourself a life makeover by investing in a professional.** If you need someone to help you create better balance, rediscover your passions, or find more fulfillment, hire a life coach. If you consistently resist exercise, hire a personal trainer. If you need to become more comfortable speaking in public, hire someone who can teach you. And so on. Spending money on bettering your life shows that you value yourself, and it will come back to you exponentially.

The person who ultimately controls how you spend your time and energy is you. Listen to the wisdom of your body and spirit. Invest wisely in yourself, and everyone around you will benefit from your joy, energy, and soulful living.

16

explore yoga

In yoga, be where you are today. You may not be where you were yesterday or where you'll be tomorrow. Be yourself. Honor where you are in this moment and let go of judgment.

—Sheryl Edsall

Part of what I love about yoga is it symbolizes so many of life's lessons. Be present. Be yourself. Let go of judgment. Connect with your higher self. You get to physically experience deeper levels of life, just by doing the poses, living in the present, and remembering to breathe.

If you want the benefits of physical exercise, be assured that yoga can be a great workout. Many professional athletes now use yoga to enhance their performance. And yoga also benefits you in ways that other exercise can't. The practice works on the glands which regulate your body functions. Inverted postures increase blood flow to your head, improving the appearance of skin and hair. You may notice your yoga instructor's beautiful skin, achieved without surgery or Botox!

Upon completing a yoga class, you are typically in a more relaxed state, more connected to your true self and your soul, more aware of your gentler self, and more joyous. Your tensions are brought down a notch. Your thoughts have more clarity. You are a more compassionate person. A lawyer friend once told me that he had to decrease his yoga workouts because he was becoming too nice to perform well in court. Do you mind becoming a more kindhearted person?

Similar to meditation, the benefits of yoga are powerful and resonate in ways you will only fully understand through experience. Here is what I can share with you about yoga:

- **find the type of yoga that works for you.** There are many types—Iyengar, vinyasa, Bikram, ashtanga, kundalini—to name some of the most popular. They are all different, and some types will appeal more to you than others. If you really want a physical workout, consider starting with Bikram (hot yoga), vinyasa, ashtanga, or power yoga. If you want a more relaxed version, try classes called "beginner" or "level one." All can be excellent workouts, though some are more aerobic than others.

- find a teacher who resonates with you. Teachers can really vary in their approach. My primary teacher, Sheryl, brings spiritual teachings into the practice, which I really appreciate. My friend Cathy, however, went to a class where the teacher described the deeper meaning of one's liver, and she ran out in fear. Some teachers are solely focused on the poses. Whatever you do, don't go to one class and then stop. Shop around. You'll find one you like.

- when you can, lower your eyes on one spot and focus on your breath during the poses. This helps you practice and enjoy the meditative benefits of yoga.

- understand and appreciate the final part, shivasana. In most classes, you will lie down at the end, focus on your breath, let it all go, and deeply relax. This is where you practice the full benefits of meditation.

- take a moment to recognize how you feel. Typically, if you were able to really let go and be present in class, you will feel energized and joyous. If you were troubled by something, you'll likely have greater clarity about your feelings and a healthier perspective. You'll be amazed at how these feelings stay with you throughout the day. You may notice that something meaningless that might have set you off before, has become just what it should be—something small to be overlooked.

- **once you understand the basics, if you can't get to a weekly class, try some yoga tapes.** My favorite tapes are created by the yoga guru Baron Baptiste, and tapes can work well if you have to miss a class. But also try to attend some classes. Yoga teachers can help with your postures and add spiritual elements that tapes may lack. They can help you narrow your focus to deepen the results. And you may feel a nice connection with others in the group when you practice yoga in class.

When practiced consistently, yoga is magical. Give it a shot. You just might appreciate your more gentle, relaxed, and compassionate self!

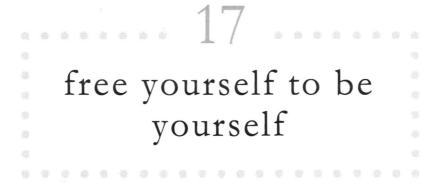

free yourself to be yourself

*To be nobody but yourself in a world which is doing its best,
day and night, to make you everybody else means to fight
the hardest battle which any human being can fight.*

—e.e. cummings

If we allow it, the unspoken pressure to be like everyone else can engulf us. If we move to a new place, we may find ourselves changing how we dress to match those around us. We may desire cars that our neighbors drive. We may mother in ways we see others doing—such as attending *every* activity and volunteer school event—because that is what "good mothering" is today. If we aren't careful, we drift away from our true self because we are letting ourselves be driven by what we see in others, rather than by our inner voice.

Many of these chapters will help you get to the core of who you are. As you work through this book, you work toward creating a balanced and authentic personal life and mommy life.

- **participate in fulfilling activities.** One mother told me that during the six months a year that she works outside the house, the little stuff doesn't bother her nearly as much. She doesn't focus on insignificant matters, such as whether her kids look perfect for school because she has other more important areas that require her attention. This doesn't mean that you have to work outside the home to be fulfilled. But it does exemplify the significance of participating in activities that are fulfilling to you. Make sure that your life consistently includes experiences that enrich you.

- **avoid pressures to parent like everyone else.** In many areas, the pressures for children to participate in numerous activities can be enormous. The intensity of training for each sport, for example, continues to start earlier in children's lives. It has become common for children as young as seven to participate in several sports and structured activities simultaneously and to rarely have a day off. Families are exhausted and countless children exhibit stress-related symptoms—headaches, stomachaches, or injuries—and may experience burnout later in life. Not to mention what is being missed by growing up with so many structured activities. If this picture doesn't feel comfortable to you, take a step back.

- **regularly revisit your values and priorities.** Not only do we need to clarify our values and ensure that our behaviors reflect them (see chapters 2 and 3), we need to do it regularly. At least twice a year, commit to reevaluating your values and how you spend your time. Stay centered on your core self. It's from this place that the real you emerges.

- **let your inner voice guide you in your parenting decisions.** Ask yourself about the range of experiences you want to offer your child. What are they naturally inclined to do? What are their individual strengths and how can you promote them? Do you want your children's self-esteem to be tightly connected to achievement or to feeling good about their efforts? How can you encourage your child to enjoy a range of healthy experiences without ignoring your own priorities? How can you structure your time so everyone grows as individuals yet you still have time to enjoy each other as a family? Step up to the challenge and answer the questions. Then make sure your lives reflect your answers.

- **let your inner voice guide you in your personal decisions.** Resist comparisons with those around you. If you feel strongly about an issue, voice it. If you want to dress differently, do it. If you think that beginning a new career in your forties or fifties is strange, think again. Be yourself. You'll begin to appreciate your courage and authenticity.

- **when you are stuck, start doing something a little differently.** If you are stuck in the same routines and living the exact same life, how are you going to evolve? When you feel stuck, start doing some things differently. If work is dull beyond belief, start focusing more on hobbies that you love. If home life bores you, get out there and have some fun, try something new, engage in a passion. Mixing it up leads to growth, and growth leads to a more meaningful life.

Let your inner voice guide you, even when it means being different. Discover and nurture what enriches you. Free yourself to be yourself. When you accomplish this, a whole new world opens up.

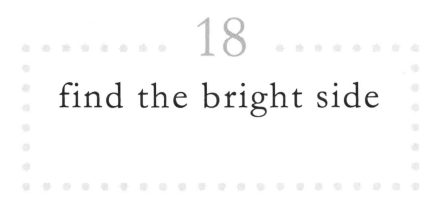

18

find the bright side

The pessimist sees difficulty in every opportunity.
The optimist sees the opportunity in every difficulty.

—Winston Churchill

We all face challenges during our lifetimes. What differentiates us is how we respond to these challenges. In the world of modern motherhood, when countless women are not feeling balanced or fulfilled, a pessimistic outlook can overtake us.

Consider these suggestions to pull yourself out of negativity and propel yourself forward:

- **find the sunny side to life's minor challenges.** We live in a culture where women constantly compare themselves to each other, often viewing themselves on the losing end of the spectrum. I give you one example that appears trivial but weighs heavily on many of our minds—our breasts! If you were fortunate/able/crazy enough (choose what works for you) to breastfeed for a long period of time, you likely observed both the deflation of and south-heading direction of your breasts. This can be quite disheartening since women's perfectly contoured breasts are in our face, daily, in all forms of media. What's a wise mother to do? Well, you can drown in pessimism and constantly feel breast-inferior. Or, you can buy some good padded bras and revel in the realization that you, in your golden years, will be lucky enough *not* to have to lug around the baggage of large breasts, all of which inevitably head south anyway. (And to the big-breasted mothers, enjoy it while you got it!) You get the picture. The perspective you take on life's minor challenges is entirely up to you.

- **find the bright side of even the biggest problems.** Research indicates that people are happier when they maintain an optimistic outlook. This doesn't advocate ignoring problems in your life. It means viewing challenges in your life as opportunities to learn something meaningful. In general, the more hurtful the experience, the more powerful the lesson. Find the lesson, the bright side, even in the most difficult situations.

- minimize your time with chronic pessimists. Some people just can't seem to escape a negative attitude about their lives—ever. These people will sap your energy. Save yourself. Choose wisely the people you spend your precious time with.

- if you are really stuck in negativity, discover what is missing. When you just can't seem to pull yourself out of the dumps, it's often a sign that something essential is missing from your life. What is it? Is it more quiet time for yourself? A deeper spiritual connection? A desire for more meaningful experiences? Spend some time asking yourself the tough questions. If you remain stuck, or are resistant to going after what you know you need, consider hiring a life coach or a counselor. Sometimes an objective professional is just what you need to dig deep into yourself, discover what is missing, and do the necessary work to create a rewarding life.

When life is challenging, search for the opportunity to learn. Find the bridge to the brighter side. And when you just can't seem to do it alone, find the courage to ask for help.

19

seek your
soul's desire

*You have to leave the city of your comfort and go into the
wilderness of your intuition. What you'll discover will
be wonderful. What you'll discover will be yourself.*

—Alan Alda

Your intuition is your soul speaking to you. When you have quieted your life, and when you really listen, your soul starts to talk. Some people go to church or a synagogue to feel a higher connection. Some people feel this connection through another avenue, such as meditation, yoga, being in nature, or writing in a journal. If you are open and you pay attention, you will discover a deeper guidance.

Consider the following:

- **your intuition taps into what something bigger wants for you.** Your intuition speaks in mysterious ways. Numerous mothers have told me about experiences they've had that seemed like strange coincidences but that guided them in some way. People often lose their jobs, for instance, only to realize that the new path they choose is more rewarding. Try to be less attached to specific outcomes and more open to the twists and turns in your life.

- **when your soul speaks, it resonates deeply if you are listening.** Sometimes what's on your mind will confuse you because it's intermingled with others' opinions and judgments. Or perhaps you are too busy to connect with your inner voice. But if you slow down your life sufficiently, create enough space for quiet and peace, and really listen to your gut, something amazing happens. Your inner self, your soul, the greater universal mind, reaches out to you and holds your greatest truth.

- **ask for guidance.** When you are really stuck—and we all are at times—ask for guidance. It doesn't matter if you are asking God or Buddha or the universe or another divine source. What matters is that you ask and that you believe in *something* bigger than yourself. And then pay attention to what happens in your life.

- **only you can act on your soul's desires.** Once you understand that things happen in your life for a reason, it's up to you to make use of the lesson. This requires that you draw upon your courage to live a meaningful life. And often this means trying something new.

It is liberating to realize that, if we let our lives unfold, our dreams will grow, our minds expand, our souls develop. What we thought twenty years ago that we'd want to "be doing" now may be very different from what we want for ourselves now. If we are open and connected to our deepest selves, what our lives will look like in twenty years may be quite different from how we imagine it now. So much is waiting for us, when we remain open to our soul's evolving desires.

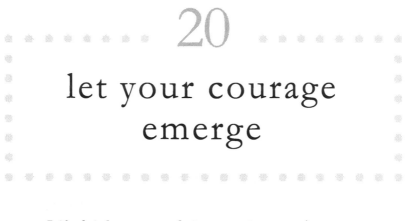

20

let your courage
emerge

Life shrinks or expands in proportion to one's courage.

—Anais Nin

Sometimes we fool ourselves into thinking that success and fulfillment in life are supposed to be easy to attain. They are not. They may come naturally, with sustained effort, but they don't come easily. And quite often, fulfilling yourself requires that you let your courage emerge; you feel your fear and do it anyway.

When I started my life-coaching business, my own coach encouraged me to send out letters to everyone I knew, introducing my new endeavor. I didn't want to. I felt uncomfortable introducing my work self to a community that, up until that time, had known my work to solely revolve around mothering. Thankfully, I felt the fear and did it regardless. Over time, referrals from friends started rolling in, and my community began to see my whole self.

Living authentically demands that you take some risks from the heart. You have a calling of some kind, in addition to your role as a mother. Now that you protect some quiet time, practice some type of spiritual connection, and regularly listen to your inner voice, you will receive some inkling about what that calling may be. And it will change over time, so keep on tuning in. It will also require you to face fears along the way. Read on for some tips on how to embrace your courage:

- **set a goal to add something authentically satisfying to your life.** This may be the steady pursuit of a dream, bringing in a new passion, balancing your life in a new way. Add something that emerges from your heart and soul, that you know instinctively is in your best interest. Perhaps it is a talent or strength that you can share with the world around you. Identify it. Then create a plan for bringing it into your life.

- **set your own pace.** As a busy mom, set up your endeavor so that your pace is realistic. Stay clear with your top priorities and maintain a healthy balance. Then keep on going.

- **keep your focus on baby steps.** I recently learned about a man who was asked how he completed the Ironman race, an unimaginably strenuous competition. He responded, "One step at a time." This is how we accomplish any large feat—with courage, sustained effort, and taking baby steps in the right direction.

- expect challenges along the way. By bringing in something new, you are changing the dynamics in your family. Challenges may appear in a variety of ways: some family members may not appreciate it if you are less available for them; you may feel uncomfortable with how your evolving life impacts others; you might feel discouraged by the self-discipline that is required; you may not like what you have to give up in order to bring your dream to fruition. We often resist change for the safety of comfort. But without change, we stop evolving; we stop living. Expect challenges along the way, and don't let fear hold you back.

- when you are trying out something big, expect big fears. Your mind might just decide to torture you. What if you don't succeed exactly as planned? Will others judge you for doing something different? What will people think of you as you experience setbacks along your journey? Acknowledge your anxiety. And do it anyway.

- reward yourself along the way. With each leap of courage, give yourself small rewards—a massage, a date with your partner, some extra time for yourself—whatever feels great to you. Keep yourself motivated, and reward your progress.

- **accept that not everyone will understand.** Not everyone is going to understand and appreciate your courage. Some, possibly your own family, might wonder when, if ever, you will be sane again. That's okay. The sooner you realize that real courage requires letting go of what other people think, the happier you will be.

- **surround yourself with support.** Limit your time with people who fuel your fears. Instead spend time with those who cheer you on.

Real success is living your life in ways that are meaningful and fulfilling to you. It involves finding your calling and sharing your strengths and talents with the world around you. You can let fear hold you back or you can embrace your courage. It's your choice. But I encourage you to choose courage, and allow your true self to come forward.

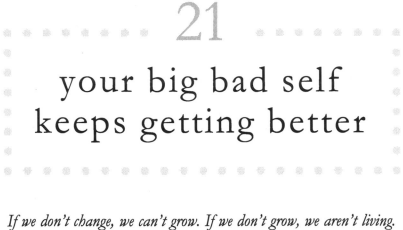

21

your big bad self keeps getting better

If we don't change, we can't grow. If we don't grow, we aren't living.

—Gail Sheehy

We tend to think of our lives in distinct patterns, as time spent with education, career, marriage, children. After we have children, and especially after we raise them, many moms mistakenly believe their options for self-development have all but disappeared. I've worked with moms in their thirties and forties who have already fallen prey to self-limiting beliefs that they can't do it because they are too old. Nothing could be further from the truth!

Quite the contrary—in many ways, life is just beginning. With age, we are wiser, more confident, and less swayed by the opinions of others. We tend to be better able to solve life's difficult challenges. We are more connected to our true selves and more comfortable in our own skin. Throughout our life span, we are blessed with the ability to reinvent ourselves over and over. Consider:

- Julia Child wrote her first best-selling book at age **forty-nine**.

- Stephanie Seymour became the first woman chief judge of the tenth Circuit Court of Appeals at age **fifty-three** (good job, mom!).

- Laura Ingalls Wilder published the first of her eight-volume Little House series at age **sixty-five**.

- Lillian Carter, Jimmy Carter's mother, joined the Peace Corps and lived in India at age **sixty-eight**.

- Jeannette Rankin, the first female member of Congress, led an antiVietnam protest on Capitol Hill at age **eighty-seven**.

- Martha Graham premiered her choreographed work the "Maple Leaf Rag" at age **ninety-six**.

And you thought life slowed down after forty? Who are you kidding? These women had the audacity to change, to grow, to be different, and to live their lives to the fullest throughout their life spans. So can you. You may choose to delay gratification of your interests and passions so you can raise your children, but don't ignore them forever! Use the wisdom and confidence you have acquired. Have the courage to try new paths. You *can* do it.

part 2

the balancing act

22

share the load

Far too many women in America are becoming sick with exhaustion and stress as they try to do things that can't—or shouldn't—be done.

—Judith Warner

If you want to live your best life, you need to make time to do activities other than caretaking, carpooling, grocery shopping, cleaning, and so on, which, if dominating the vast majority of your "free" time, will drain and exhaust you. You must be able to resist any pressures that you need to "do it all" to be a successful mom. If you keep trying to uphold the impossible supermom syndrome, you may very well be running on empty and find yourself nodding your head in recognition when you hear that 70 percent of mothers report motherhood is "incredibly stressful."

Thankfully, there is a way out! If you free up some time for your priorities and you share the load at home, your life will become more manageable. Give up some control and learn to share the responsibilities. Hire assistance where you can, ask your partner to help, and require help from your children. They will learn the valuable life lessons of responsibility and independence while freeing up some crucial time and energy for you.

How to share the load? Here are some tips:

- **give each child at least two or three chores to do daily.** Two- to four-year-olds can help set the table, pick up toys, and dress themselves. Children five and older can do tasks such as carry out the trash, feed animals, set and clear the table, help with cooking, and make their beds. Teenagers can take over full duties such as planning and cooking a meal, cleaning the kitchen after dinner, and laundry.

- **ask your partner to help more.** Talk with your partner, if you have one, about sharing more responsibilities at home. There *are* ways to share more parenting and household responsibilities; you just might need to get creative. For instance, if your husband leaves early for work, ask him to do the dishes at night and put the kids to bed. If he works late, ask him to stay home some mornings to help with that hectic routine. On the weekends, take turns giving each other some time off from child care and household responsibilities.

- **help your spouse appreciate your hard work at home.** Mothers who don't have a relatively equal parenting balance with their partners have told me (regardless if they work outside the home or not) that their partners believe they should feel satisfied, rather than overwhelmed, with their vast mommy duties. If you are in this situation, arrange for one day off each weekend, and let your partner do all the child care, cooking, cleaning, and shopping. You'll be surprised how quickly minds can change!

- **hire help.** Moms are often reluctant to do this, but help with the duties that wear you down, such as cleaning and laundry, can make a world of difference. If you really feel you can't afford more help, please read chapter 29 before you close your mind on this subject.

Some interesting dynamics occur when you share more responsibilities with others. As you fill the extra time with meaningful activities, such as pursuing a passion or interest, or taking good care of yourself, you will become more of the person you really want to be. You are demonstrating that you value yourself, just as you value the rest of your family. You rediscover energy you forgot you had. You are happier. And, in turn, everyone in the family benefits.

23

just say no

Once you get rid of the idea that you must please other people before you please yourself, and you begin to follow your own instincts—only then can you be successful. You become more satisfied, and when you are, other people tend to be satisfied by what you do.

—Raquel Welch

Something we are often guilty of is saying yes, when we really want to say no. Why do we do this? Maybe it's because we don't want to disappoint someone, or because we feel like we have to "do it all" to be respected and valued. If you fall into this trap, take a step back and recognize that if you want balance and inner peace, you must be able to just say no to what is not on your highest-priorities list.

Here are some suggestions:

- **when you are asked to do something, take time to think through your highest priorities and don't answer right away.** Take at least twenty-four hours to think about it. Is it on your highest-priorities list (see chapter 3)? Is it something you really have time to do and still keep a healthy balance and some downtime? If not, just say no!

- **realize you will, at times, disappoint others.** You can't please people all the time and still be good to yourself. Sometimes you need to say no to others, in order to say yes to yourself.

- **if you are stuck in the "I have to do it all cuz I'm Supermama" trap, recognize it and let it go.** When you are frantic, you block your ability to live your life to the fullest. You give less to yourself and your family because you have less to give. In essence, you diminish your ability to enjoy and feel good about your life. Now, why would you want to do that?

- **keep explanations to a minimum.** Sometimes we add unnecessary stress to our lives by obsessing about the ideal way to get out of something. Save your energy for more important projects. A simple "Thanks for asking, but I just can't add that into my life right now" is great. If the other person doesn't understand, recognize that for what it is—their problem, not yours!

By being able to just say no, you will free up time to bring in what matters most in your life. You will be able to live more peacefully and authentically. Liberate yourself and start practicing this one today!

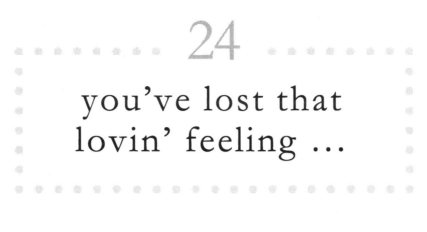

24

you've lost that lovin' feeling ...

Love is not effortless. To the contrary, love is effortful.

—M. Scott Peck

most parents, with their decision to raise a family together, have made a commitment to do their best to live "happily ever after" with their partners. If your children become the sole focus in your family, you risk disconnecting from each other and overindulging your children. If, however, you choose to devote weekly time to each other as a couple, you are investing in the long-term health of your relationship. You are also demonstrating to your children what a healthy, loving adult relationship requires—time and attention to each other. Furthermore, children feel safe and secure when their parents have a strong bond together.

Nurture your primary relationship. Consider these tips:

- **choose a weekly date night.** Once a week, devote the evening or a period of time solely to you and your life partner. Go out to dinner, take a walk and have a picnic, ride bikes together, go to the gym and have coffee afterwards. Choose activities that fit into your budget and help you both connect.

- **rediscover your common interests.** What brought you together in the first place? What do you enjoy doing together? Rediscover your common interests, and weave them into your date night. Go to a museum or play tennis. One of my client's "date nights" is actually hiking on Sunday afternoons with her husband. Get creative and renew your sense of adventure together.

- **keep it light and enjoyable.** The goal is to connect and enjoy each other. My husband and I have learned not to talk about family dramas or financial issues on date night. Figure out your off-limits areas and save the potentially stressful conversations for another time.

- **make it regular.** One of the greatest challenges to modern parenthood is making time for each other ... consistently. You will notice that many other seemingly essential activities or events will try hard to steal you away. Don't let them. Get this on your highest-priorities list (see chapter 3) and, short of sick kids or a funeral, protect your weekly dates.

- **make it fun for your kids.** Most children love babysitters who are fun and consistent in their lives. Simplify your life and give your kids that consistency by asking the same sitter to commit to your date time every week. Whether it is a loving relative or energetic teenager, leave behind plenty of ideas for fun. Over time, your children will come to enjoy your time away as much as you do!

Take time to rekindle that lovin' feeling. Have fun together. Maintain a strong connection over the years, and you'll have something remaining when the only people left in your home are you two!

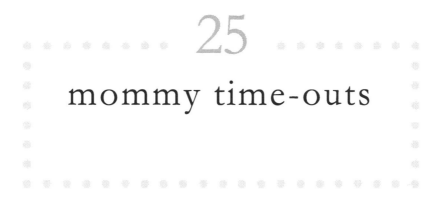

25

mommy time-outs

When my kids become wild and unruly, I use a nice, safe playpen.
When they're finished, I climb out.

—Erma Bombeck

arenting is hard work. We often find ourselves in full-speed mode, thinking that if we go-go-go, we'll get more done, be more productive, be more successful. However, research has demonstrated that we function optimally when we intersperse periods of full-speed mode with recovery breaks. We actually accomplish more when we structure in some downtime. To work at their best, our brains and bodies physically demand rest and renewal.

Whether you work outside the home or not, you work hard. Just as corporate executives and top-ranked athletes have learned, if you constantly operate in full-speed mode, you ultimately sacrifice too much. Your body is likely to warn you that you are overdoing it. You may start to feel scattered and sluggish. Brain functions start to slow. Perhaps you start sentences that you can't finish because you can't remember what you were talking about. Sound familiar? If you still push ahead at full-speed, your body talks to you with more debilitating ailments, such as exhaustion, illness, insomnia, or depression. Don't get to this point. If you are headed in this direction, or are already there, repair yourself by scheduling in recovery breaks immediately.

Intersperse your full-speed mode with time-outs, and life will get a whole lot better. Consider these tips:

- **plan your days with at least one time-out before lunch and before dinner.** These breaks can be anything that removes you from your daily duties and rests your brain. Sitting still to breathe deeply, yoga, short naps, or a walk in the sunshine are all excellent choices.

- **make your exercise routine part of your recovery time.** If you sprint to the crowded, noisy gym and crank out some weights while constantly watching the clock, you may not be revitalizing yourself. If you exercise without strict time demands, however, your experience can be a break from your daily grind. Create exercise routines that are stress-free rather than stressful.

- **take at least a half day, every week, of unstructured "me time."** Yes, you can! Shift your perspective to understand that it's essential to take this time for yourself. A time for no plans and no schedules of any kind. You get to do what you feel like doing, rather than what your busy schedule demands. If you want to stay in your pajamas or lounge in the bathtub, feel free! In our era of constant motion, it really is imperative that you consistently take some time to rest your brain and separate from all the demands. Start this now and you'll feel better immediately.

- **periodically take an extended break from it all.** There are times when we all need a longer escape from daily stresses to help us connect with our authentic selves and identify our true passions and life goals. This may be achieved with an overnight hotel stay, a three-day retreat somewhere, or even a couple of weeks alone. The amount of time you need depends on how imbalanced you feel and the coverage you can arrange for your children at home. The aim of your extended break is to be on your own, unplug yourself from the outside world, and reconnect with yourself again.

When you start incorporating recovery breaks into your daily life, you'll likely notice the difference immediately. You gain a better perspective on your life and the smaller stresses are put in their smaller place. You may still be a busy bee, like I am, but you'll feel more centered and energized. Your choices are more likely to reflect what you really want, because you are making fewer choices on autopilot and more with a clearer head. Remind yourself that you need to take time-outs to adequately care for yourself and function at your best.

26

bring in the fun!

Somebody's boring me; I think it's me.

—Dylan Thomas

have you ever noticed that moms are usually the ones who forego having fun? We'll run ourselves ragged to make sure our kids get to numerous activities and parties and to give our partners their much-needed time to relax and have fun. At the end of the week, we often find ourselves where we started—worn out and seriously lacking in good times.

Like everyone else, we need to have some fun to help us enjoy our lives and maintain a healthy perspective. Here are some ideas to get you started:

- **reinvent the fun you had as a child.** What did you really love to do as a child and how can you recreate it now? If you loved playing soccer, for instance, join a team, start a team, or coach your daughter! If you loved playing the piano, take lessons again and entertain your family. Get creative.

- **rediscover the magic of play with your children.** Most children instinctively play and create fun in their lives. Try joining in hide-and-seek, basketball, goofing around in the pool, or whatever else your kids are doing. If they are under twelve, they'll likely love having you involved, and you may find it's genuinely fun! (Skip this if they are older and you are met with "Get a life, mom!" Such responses will squash the fun.)

- **exhibit your inner silliness!** I've learned from my husband and his mother that some adults are naturally gifted in their playfulness. At a business meeting, my mother-in-law dressed up as Little Bo Peep and entertained the crowd, just to keep it lively! Okay. Perhaps that doesn't sound like fun to you. However, something else must: dancing in public, teaching your kids jokes, belting out tunes in the shower, skipping with your kids when you shop …

- **start a group with other like-minded, fun people.** I have a friend who joined a "mystery group" of twelve women, each of whom plans a fun, surprise event each month. I'm in an investment group that's heavy on the laughter and mild on the investing. What can you join or start that would be fun?

- **sign up for a class that sounds like fun.** Think about what you already enjoy or what might be new and exciting. Asian cooking? Latin dancing? Surfing? Speaking Italian? Think outside the box. One of my clients recently took a hula-dancing class!

- **budget in and schedule vacations.** Do what you can afford and what brings a smile to your face. Exploring a new culture? Skiing? A wilderness adventure? Lounging in the sun? Vacations can be a great escape from life stresses, a wonderful way to reconnect with yourself, your partner, or your family, and an excellent way to enhance your mood when you return.

Lifting your spirits also lifts your family's spirits. You've got one shot at this life. Make sure you enjoy it, and bring in the fun!

27

the family CEO
gets organized

*Of course I'd like to be the ideal mother.
But I'm too busy raising children.*

—comic by Bill Keane

i don't know many people who love scheduling and organizing their families. For most of us, it's part of the drudgery of motherhood. As families grow and chaos multiplies, if you are totally disorganized, you'll likely find yourself throwing your hands in the air, wondering why you signed on for this job at all. But if you take the time to get more organized, your short-term pain is well worth the peace of mind.

Here are some tips for organizing your lively brood:

- **keep your priorities clear.** Make sure you are only including in your family lives what you really believe belongs there. Continually revisit your highest-priorities list (see chapter 3) and get your family priorities on the schedule, including downtime, interactive family time, and one-on-one time with each child. If your family grows, your decisions about what to bring in and what to leave out will be affected not only by individual needs but by the greater family needs. Since there are a limited number of hours in a day, your expertise in saying no will definitely come in handy as you protect your highest priorities and let the smaller stuff go.

- **sometimes less is more.** In our era of overdrive, it's easy to get lost in all the "to do" lists. Parents talk about wanting to expose their children to everything to help determine what they like best. The problem is, most activities have become very time-consuming. When you expose them to too much, your children miss out on non-structured experiences and risk becoming exhausted, injured, or burned out. Consider limiting your child's activities to a few that they like, or rotate activities over the years and liberate all of you to live more balanced, peaceful lives.

- **give each child their own "cubbie" and bulletin board.** Try to arrange separate areas for summer and camp stuff, winter stuff, and school necessities. Every child puts their shoes, hats, swim goggles, and whatever else they need to bring in and out of the house into their cubbie areas. Hang separate bulletin boards for each child's prized works of art, invitations, and other critical information. Creating different spaces for each child can go a long way toward containing clutter and maintaining some sense of order.

- **make time to update schedules in one family calendar.** Set aside time, at least twice a week, to update schedules for car pools, activities, lunches, parties, babysitter times, and anything else that is helpful. Consider giving a separate ink color, as my friend Sharon does, to each child and parent. Some mothers like to write out their dinner plans, including when their partner or one of the kids is the chef or when takeout is in order. As children get older, ask them to regularly update their own schedules with you, as well as on the family calendar.

- **the morning routine is best started the night before.** Parents usually dread morning mayhem. Try to do as much as possible the night before. For instance, have children help make lunches, get out their clothes, have homework completed and put away, even organize breakfast, the night before. You'll be amazed at how much this one simple step can make a world of difference in how you all start your days.

- **schedule in time to respond.** When you are busy, let the answering machine get the phone. You aren't doing anyone any favors when you frantically pick up the phone only to bellow, "I can't talk to you right now!" Diffuse the drama by returning calls, and e-mails, at a more convenient time.

- **don't forget to include some fun with mom!** Make sure you get in some quality, weekly fun time with each child. Remember, what your children will recall with fondness are those interactive moments with you—not how they participated in four activities at once, thanks to your super scheduling talents. Just as dads tend to work in the fun with their kids, so can you. Look for a balance here and everyone will benefit.

- **if you parent with a significant other, you need a weekly business meeting.** This is a time to review your schedules together and determine who does what and when. Share the parenting responsibilities wherever possible. Check to ensure that how your family spends their time reflects your core values. This is also a good occasion to discuss the tough issues, such as problems you are having with each other, with the children, or with finances.

- **allow for extra time.** Try to give yourself an extra five or ten minutes for traffic, spilled juice, an empty gas tank, the associate who is late with her assignment, and so on. There are situations in life you can't control. If you build in a little extra time to get from point A to point B, you'll be much more able to relax and arrive at your next destination with a smile.

- **when you're in survival mode, take it all down a notch.** My friend Amy offered an excellent idea for the times you are in "survival mode," such as when you have a newborn infant or a chronically sick family member. Every day, decide on one thing to do for your children, one thing to do for the management of the household, and one thing to do for yourself. In this manner, you are simplifying at a time when simplifying is essential. You can add in more obligations and activities as your situation changes.

When you dedicate time to get organized and make decisions based on your true priorities, your family lives become manageable. And rather than constantly wasting energy on loose ends, you liberate yourself to spend more time on other areas of your life that matter too.

28

money matters

We can tell our values by looking at our checkbook stubs.

—Gloria Steinem

I've talked to countless moms who bury their head in the sand when it comes to money. The problem is, you can't function too well in the sand. With head buried, our relationship with money can create all kinds of insidious problems. On the other hand, if you consciously shift the way you spend money to better reflect your values, you can enhance your life enormously. It's your choice.

Contrary to what you may believe, you are capable of taking charge of your financial health. Not only would you need to be able to take care of yourself if you were to find yourself on your own, now or in the future, but you also need to demonstrate to yourself and to your children that you are a fully functioning, competent individual who can stand on her own two feet in this world. So, pull your head out of the sand and get your finances in order. Here are some tips to get you going:

- **know your family's income.** How much money flows into your lives? Not certain? Get certain. Write down exactly how much income you and a partner, if you have one, bring in after taxes are paid. Add in any other sources of annual income as well, such as interest on financial accounts.

- **get a grip on your expenses.** Yes, you can do this too. If you don't know where your money goes, write down exactly what you and your family spend for the next month. Everything. Then compare this number to your last three months of credit card bills and bank account statements to ensure that you have an accurate estimate of your monthly expenses. Multiply this number by twelve. Now, add 5 percent to this number to allow for unexpected expenses, such as the extra doctor bills that result when your kids stick vitamins in their ears instead of their mouths. This number is a reasonable estimate of your annual expenses.

- **subtract the two and discover your annual savings.** In the simplest of terms, the amount going out, subtracted from the amount coming in, is your savings. Financial guru David Bach encourages us to save 12 percent of our gross yearly income (the amount coming in before taxes are taken out) on retirement savings. If what you save is less than this amount—and most people save less than this—figure out how to save more. Notice that how much you make matters less than how much you spend.

- **if you need to spend less in order to save more, separate your needs from your wants.** Study your expenditures and categorize them into needs or wants. Be honest. (Although you may beg to differ, the mortgage is a need; your third leather bag is a want). Study your want list and determine what you can decrease. For instance, do you really need five lattes a week, at $80 a month, or can you make your coffee at home? Can you live without two pedicures a month and save the $50? Can you commit to only buying clothes you'll really wear frequently and buy them only on sale? Are you consistently using your gym, or can you cancel the membership and regularly meet friends for a walk or jog? Why not plan vacations ahead of time and benefit from discounted Web fares?

- **make sure your spending reflects your range of values.** When you keep track of your expenditures, how you spend money transforms from something potentially unconscious to something real and tangible. Ask yourself, how does your spending reflect your values? For example, if you value quality time with your children but they are never around because they are constantly involved in structured activities (which costs money), perhaps the number of activities you have your kids signed up for doesn't properly reflect your values. Or, if you value giving money to those who are less fortunate, but you spend all the money you make, it seems you are neglecting this value. The more values you neglect, the less fulfilling your life. How can you rearrange your expenditures to better reflect your values? Write down your ideas and start implementing them.

- **if you need to spend less, spend only cash.** The best way to avoid spending money you don't have is to avoid spending money you don't have! Credit cards can fool you into thinking you have money that you don't. If this is a problem for you, cut up the cards and use cash.

- **use your community resources.** Instead of buying books, take your kids to the library and borrow books. Some libraries also lend out computer programs, movies, and puzzles. Many towns have community programs that provide athletic or educational classes for a nominal fee. Do some research and teach your kids the value of using community resources to save money.

- **create a MOM (mama's own money) budget.** Financial disagreements are cited as one of the most common causes of divorce. Lessen the money wars in your relationship by carving out your own budget. Agree on a MOM budget for whatever you want to spend your money on. A spouse might find your fourth pair of black shoes frivolous, but since you are honest and stay within the agreed-upon

boundaries of your MOM budget, you can buy whatever item or self-care service you want—without guilt. Just make sure it fits into your overall family plan of spending less than you make and saving for your future.

- **if you want a larger family income and you don't work for pay, consider it.** Provided your children are well cared for while you work, consider working at least part-time if you are blessed with the choice. There are countless benefits to getting paid for something you love to do. Think about your passions—gardening, writing, sports, cooking, arranging flowers, politics, communicating with others—and how you can turn them into a payment. If you open yourself to the possibilities and are willing to work hard, you can do it.

- **it's not as hard as you might think.** Taking charge of your finances might feel scary at first, but it's actually quite liberating. By developing an honest relationship with money and spending money on what you value, you live with integrity. That's a whole lot better than living in denial or with guilt!

Money does matter. As a busy mom, this is one area you can't afford to neglect. So get over any issues you have with spending money wisely. Get your financial life in order by understanding your family's sources of income and focusing your spending on what really matters to you, including saving responsibly for your future. Remember, the more your sources of income are derived from real passions and interests, and the more your spending reflects your values and allows you to live the life you want, the more fulfilling your life.

29

feeling great about affording help

I hope that the way you spend your money is in line with the truth of who you are and what you care about.

—Oprah

how can we get help for our domestic duties and feel great about it? It's a real challenge for moms who are trapped in the overparenting pressures of our modern society. The expectations to be attentive to our children's every move, combined with countless other responsibilities and duties we take on, have reached a frenzied level. Affordable options for child care are often of marginal quality. For the most part, our society is no longer designed so that our communities or extended families assist with raising our children. And if we are raising children with spouses, many are highly focused on their

work during the week and often unavailable to help with the daily responsibilities of child care and managing a household.

To make matters worse, we may unintentionally contribute to the problem, rather than the solution, by buying into it all. We tend to be hard on ourselves when it comes to asking for help. We've bought into the notion that we need to do it all. I have worked with many moms who say they can't achieve their personal dreams, outside of their children, because they can't afford more help with their domestic lives and they can't expect their partners to do more. However, after evaluating their real choices and aligning their purchasing decisions with their genuine values, these women have realized that they *can* afford more help. In doing so, they've been able to create happier and fuller lives.

It's worth wading through the obstacles to demonstrate to yourself and your family that your sanity does matter. Your personal goals and ambitions *do* matter. Prioritizing, managing your money to reflect your deepest values, and arranging some help to allow you to focus some time on yourself is truly an honorable way to live. Consider these tips to get you going or keep you on track:

- if you feel like you can't afford enough help to allow you to live a balanced, fulfilling life, reevaluate your expenses. How can you reduce your expenses to allow your spending to better reflect your own needs? If hiring some help with your kids or domestic duties will free you up to achieve your dreams and live a more rewarding life, isn't that a noble cause? Refer to the exercises and advice in chapter 28.

- **stop sacrificing personal goals and a fulfilling life for material possessions.** I've listened to many moms who say they don't want to spend money on a housekeeper or babysitter but are just too exhausted by "doing it all" that they can't focus on their own needs. These same moms wear expensive clothes and drive luxury cars. You may not be in this boat, but you get the idea. How you spend your money needs to reflect your values. If you value the idea of living a whole, balanced life, your spending needs to reflect this. Translated into practical terms, if you tend to neglect your personal needs, cut the material expenses and hire some help.

- **focus on getting help for areas that drain your energy.** Consider a low-cost adolescent "mother's helper" to help chase the kids while you attend to personal pursuits or organize dinner. Perhaps a teenager can mow your lawn, walk the dog, or do some filing for you. Maybe a babysitter can do your laundry or grocery shop. Get creative!

- **if you've cut unnecessary expenses and it's still too difficult to pay for the help you need to feel balanced, get creative.** Do you have friends who would swap some babysitting time with you? Is your partner really doing his/her fair share of domestic duties? Research shows that it is more exhausting to stay home all day, raise kids, and manage the household than it is to go to "work." So, the general feeling that the one who is gone longer for paid work should do less around the house when s/he's at home doesn't fly! What else can your children do to help around the house? Record how you spend your waking hours and discuss with your partner how this time may be more equally divided.

- **spend quality time with your children to maintain a good relationship.** Several chapters in this book will help you ensure that you regularly spend quality time with your children. Maintaining a close, healthy relationship with them will help you both feel more secure about accepting help from others.

Invest in your whole self and you truly will live a life of abundance. To accomplish this, you will likely need to arrange for some help, even if that means spending some money. In doing so, you are demonstrating that you truly value yourself as a dynamic individual. In turn, your children are more likely to value and invest in their own unique selves as they grow into adulthood. Get the help you need, spend your extra time on nurturing and fulfilling yourself, and enjoy the deeply satisfying life you deserve.

30

become a stellar communicator

People would rather be listened to, than talked to.

—Tom Coburn

how we communicate has a lot to do with how we share ourselves with the world and how we build relationships with others. It is our bridge to our family members and to the world around
us. Spend some time working on your communication. Learn to listen
extremely well. Remain open-minded and try to be flexible about
occasionally altering your beliefs, as long as they remain aligned with
your authentic self. Develop healthy boundaries. Share your own
thoughts and feelings with pride, even when they differ from someone else's.

Here are some suggestions to help you become a stellar communicator:

- **become a fabulous listener.** I've gotten myself in trouble too many times by reacting to a situation before I listened really well. Listen before you respond—without blame, judgments, or interruptions. Maintain eye contact. Search for a genuine understanding of others' feelings and thoughts. Reflect your understanding of what they are saying. Focus on listening more than talking. Becoming a fabulous listener can transform poor communication and improve relationships like nothing else.

- **when it's your turn to talk about a problem or issue, focus on your feelings and thoughts.** Talk about how a situation or behavior makes you feel. Use "I statements" and steer clear of blame. For instance, to your partner, you might say, "I feel frustrated when you ignore the dishes because I feel like I need to do them for you or they won't get done." Then listen to his perspective and brainstorm solutions together.

- **get comfortable with voicing your differences.** For the mothers out there who are fearful of expressing a different opinion, stand up and be heard! Part of feeling great about who you are is sharing who you are with others. You aren't being true to yourself if you are constantly silencing yourself. There are times when it's better not to jump in with an opinion, such as in heated arguments when no one is really listening anyway. But, there are plenty of times when it's important to share your voice. Don't miss these opportunities. Sharing opinions is what allows us to learn from each other, to understand each other better, and to grow closer. It's essential to be real with others if you want to be close to them. So rise above the fear, start talking, and accept that differences are inevitable.

- **recognize that nonverbal communication can be powerful.** *How* you say something is often more important than *what* you say. When I got to where I would rarely raise my voice in an argument with my husband, but I would still flail my hands all around—with the defense, "I'm Italian!" (third generation) and "Italians use their hands!"—I realized he would just shut down. As challenging as it has been for me, I now really try to express myself calmly, toning down my body language as well. The other person listens better when we remain calm. It's that simple.

- **get clear with your boundaries.** Your boundaries are healthy limits that you set with others. If people overstep your boundaries, such as by treating you in ways you consider disrespectful, let them know how you feel. No one can walk over you without your permission. And if no one knows what your boundaries are, how can they avoid breaking them? You have to explain your boundaries, such as by saying, "If someone is yelling at me, I don't listen until they calm down," or

"I don't answer my phone after 6 P.M., so I can focus on my family. If you call after then, my machine will answer and I'll call you back the next day or as soon as I can." Be clear and consistent with your boundaries, and people will catch on.

- **deal with the big problems directly.** If you have a problem with someone, go directly to the source. Skip the gossip. Don't waste your energy obsessing about whether it's okay or not to confront the person. Calmly express how you feel. And then listen to how the other person feels. This is how honest communication occurs, differences get aired, and real relationships develop.

- **when you lose control, apologize.** Never underestimate the power of saying you are sorry. If your emotions get heated and you end up overreacting or freaking out, calm yourself down and apologize. Then figure out where you went wrong, remind yourself how to do it differently next time, and move on.

- **if you find yourself consistently overreacting, look at the imbalances in your life.** Pay attention if you are irritable with others on a regular basis. Is something out of balance in your life? What might be missing? Do you have enough downtime ... spiritual time ... alone time ... exercise ... fun ... passions and interests? Odds are you don't. Correcting the balance might be just what you need so you can communicate better with the world around you.

- if you are hiring someone, in or out of the home, clearly express your expectations and communicate well. Think through the job requirements before you hire someone. If you are hiring a babysitter, do you also expect housekeeping to be a part of the job? If so, what exactly do you want the person to do? Once you are clear with what your needs are, make sure you are hiring the employee for enough hours to be able to successfully meet them. Check in every now and then, express gratitude for jobs done well, and openly discuss any problem areas. Working relationships require some work. Do your part to communicate well.

- remove yourself from discussions that get out of control. Sometimes emotions get the better of us and we get away from healthy conversations. If voices are escalating and people are no longer listening to each other, it's unhealthy. End it. Change the subject or walk away until the air is calm again.

How we communicate affects so many dimensions of our lives—our self-worth, our relationships, our work, our parenting. To live your best life, consciously improve how you converse with others and strive to become a stellar communicator.

31

from work mode to mommy mode

To do two things at once is to do neither.

—Publilius Syrus

If you work, in addition to parenting, try to keep it separate from the rest of your life. When you blend the two, you are inviting stress into your world. Neither benefits, not your kids or your work, from your scattered attention. Consider these tips to help you successfully separate work life from the rest of your life:

- **create a separate work space in your home.** If you work at home, get a separate phone line and work area. If you don't have an office space, convert another room, such as a guest room, to double as your office. (And don't let guests stay there during your work hours).

- **set distinct work times when you are unavailable to your family or friends.** If you work for yourself or in your home, it's crucial that you define and stick to your work hours. Don't return personal calls or clean the kitchen during this time. Focus on your work. You'll be much more productive.

- **invest time in yourself before your family wakes up in the morning.** It can be incredibly peaceful to work for a couple of hours before your family rises. Much of this book was written between five and seven o'clock in the morning. Start going to bed earlier, and try it. Once your body adjusts, you may find that it's the time of day you are most focused, creative, and productive. If work is not an option in the early hours, think about getting in some quality time for other areas of your life, such as exercise or spiritual practices.

- **before you switch to mommy mode, center yourself.** I can't stress this one enough. Your children would much rather you take extra time for yourself than to have you return to them stressed about work. Center yourself first. Before you leave work, write down what needs to be completed next time, and then focus on letting it go. Breathe deeply for five or ten minutes. Unwind during a commute.

Rejoin your family refreshed and ready to handle whatever comes your way.

- **if the transition is still difficult, try exercising in between.** Many men have discovered the benefits of exercising before returning home, and so can you. If you can't seem to wind down enough to enter mommy mode peacefully, go for a walk, hit the gym for thirty minutes, or catch a yoga class. Brief exercise may be just what you need to let go of the tension from work.

Separate work from the rest of your life, and center yourself in between the two. When you accomplish this, you'll feel happier and more successful in both work mode and mommy mode.

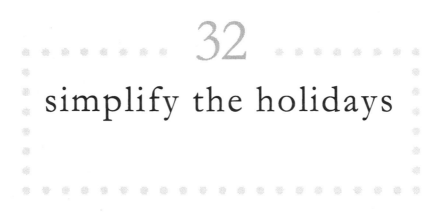

32

simplify the holidays

I don't know the key to success, but the key to
failure is trying to please everybody.

—Bill Cosby

a s a busy mother, the key to a joyous holiday is to prioritize and keep it simple. If you think back to your fondest holiday memories as a child, they probably are related to some expression of love. They probably are not related to memories of stressed out, crazed, lunatic behaviors by mothers frantically trying to do it all and please everyone.

To shift your focus to what really matters, consider these suggestions:

- delegate! If you are hosting, ask others to bring food or, if your budget allows, cater at least some of the meal. If you have friends or relatives who need to have that home-cooked holiday meal, cheerfully announce that you would love to serve *their* home-cooked food any time they want to bring it!

- keep decorations simple. Not every house on the block needs to progress through the plethora of Halloween-Thanksgiving-Christmas/Hanukkah/Kwanzaa decorations. Unless you are really passionate about decorating, be the one to do less. Others will appreciate you for it!

- reconsider holiday cards. These take a lot of time and energy. If you enjoy the concept of sending cards, as I do, think through your options: send them every other year, send only to out-of-town friends, or send them for Valentine's Day, when life isn't as busy.

- think about how to teach your deepest values to your children. Most of us want our children to learn about giving to others, not just receiving. Holidays, when our kids receive so much, are an excellent time to teach about the gift of giving. Ask your kids to donate some of their allowance or holiday money to charities. Think about giving to charities in honor of family members. (Does Uncle Jim really need another tie?)

- limit gifts, create a budget, and stick to it. This doesn't mean create a budget and then fake short-term dementia to forget it! Remember your commitment to stay aligned with your values by spending money wisely and sticking to a holiday budget. Your children will genuinely appreciate quality time with happy parents more than they will a myriad of gifts.

- **create meaningful traditions.** What do you want to do together as a family? Attend a temple, church, or create your own spiritual ceremony? Spend time together decorating the tree, singing on the block, or working at a soup kitchen? Why not light a candle every night in December to show gratitude for your good fortune, acknowledging that many people don't have the luxury of electricity? Don't limit yourself to the traditions you've always known. Start your own!

I encourage you to spend your energy in the areas that you care most about, and simplify the rest. This will free you up to live your life the way you want to and to create meaningful holiday experiences.

part 3

your fabulous family

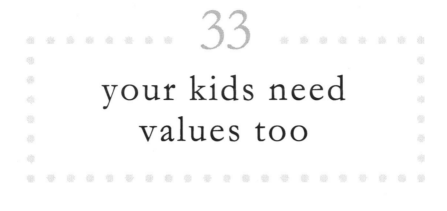

your kids need
values too

*The most pathetic person in the world is someone
who has sight, but no vision.*

—Helen Keller

In earlier chapters, I've encouraged you to become more conscious
of how your lives take shape—to connect with your values and
ensure that how you spend your energy reflects these values. Make
sure your kids do it too.

Begin by setting an excellent example. If you just talk the talk
without walking the walk, you're wasting your time. Demonstrate
your healthy self-esteem by ensuring that your inside world, your
beliefs and feelings, are aligned with your outside world, your behavior. Then provide ample experiences for your children to observe

your values, develop their own, and align their behaviors with these ideals.

- **write down at least seven values that you hope to instill in your child.** Think through a wide range of values that are important to you. Some examples are compassion for others, gratitude, a love of learning, confidence, empathy, spirituality, living in the present, helping others, creativity, leadership, courage, maintaining balance, and independence. Make a complete list and post it somewhere where you can see it frequently.

- **create specific ways to help promote these values.** Support your values with a variety of experiences. If you believe in the power of gratitude, create some rituals together that help your children appreciate their lives. If you value courage, encourage them to try something new. If you value compassion and a desire to help others, offer a choice of charitable experiences your child can participate in. To get started, check out www.charities.org, www.womenforwomen.org, www.volunteermatch.org, and www.familycares.org.

- **explore the feelings that arise from these experiences.** If you've worked together to help others who are less fortunate, how does your child feel about it? Help him recognize that it feels good to help others. If your kids are able to connect positive feelings with their experiences, they are more likely to internalize the deeper meaning, the true value, of the experience.

- **teach them to trust their own intuition.** Help your child learn to listen to her gut, her own inner voice. If something makes her uncomfortable, encourage her to talk about it. Help her learn to distinguish between the fear of something new, which is generally *not* a reason to avoid something, from something that her gut says isn't right, which *is* a reason to avoid something. We are all born with an innate ability to know when something just isn't right for us. Help your kids listen to and trust their intuition.

- **respect and appreciate your children's values as they develop.** It's not important that their values entirely match yours. What's important is that your children become mindful of their own values. If your child cherishes adventure and you don't, you still need to encourage this part of her. Respecting their ideals and interests helps your children learn to live *their* lives authentically.

- **use their natural strengths and interests to teach values.** One of the biggest parenting challenges can be accepting that our children are not miniatures of ourselves. You may have learned the value of teamwork through sports, while your child may want to experience working with others in a school play. If your creativity is expressed through music, hers may be expressed in writing. If you have found organized religion to be a major source of strength in your life, accept that your child may discover her spirituality elsewhere, such as in nature or through yoga or meditation. Accept these differences and use your children's natural strengths and interests as pathways to teach values.

- **if you consistently want more for your children than you want for yourself, focus more on yourself.** Some moms are so involved in giving their child everything, they disconnect from their own needs. Children don't deserve more than you do. You both deserve amazing, fulfilling, and rewarding lives. Focus more on defining and achieving personal goals; your children will benefit tremendously by observing you live your best life.

- **make it happen.** Thinking about all of this is not enough. You need to do it. Look at the upcoming year. How are you going to teach a variety of good values to your kids?

Help your children live enriching lives by practicing your values, helping them develop their own, and encouraging them to trust their intuition. Help them create a vision for *how* they want to be and *who* they want to be. In doing so, you are helping them build the foundation for a truly meaningful, authentic life.

34

don't micro-mommy

Too many of us now allow ourselves to be defined by motherhood and direct every ounce of our energy into our children. This sounds noble on the surface but in fact it's doing no one—not ourselves, or our children—any good.

—Judith Warner

It's easy to fall into the trap of feeling guilty about focusing your attention on areas other than your children. Many of us spend endless hours, whether we work outside the home or not, trying to immediately attend to our children's every perceived need; solve every issue that arises; get our children into countless scheduled sports and other activities, regardless of our own or their exhaustion;

and be a part of as many school and after-school events (their time away from us) that we possibly can.

We are stepping in and running the lives of our children much more than previous generations did—and at what cost? We risk running ourselves ragged and feeling depressed or anxious. Our children, guinea pigs in this experiment, risk being overindulged, incapable of handling age-appropriate responsibilities and managing life stresses, and eventually unhappy with how they feel the real world treats them.

It's not easy to resist the current pressures to devote our entire lives to our children, but it's a lot easier if we remind ourselves of how unhealthy these behaviors actually are. Consider the following:

- **give your child age-appropriate chores and responsibilities, even if you can do it yourself or hire the help to do it.** Whether you do the work or you've hired some help, the result is the same. You risk overindulging your children, who may grow up thinking the world should take care of them. They are in for quite a shock when the world doesn't agree. Gain a solid understanding of age-appropriate chores and put them to use. Most four-year-olds can dress themselves. Most children as young as seven are perfectly capable of making their own lunches. What about asking your kids to help with dinner, do their homework on their own, or watch a younger sibling for a short period of time when you are busy?

- **resist the temptation to immediately drop everything to attend to your child's every perceived need.** If you meet your child's every perceived need, you are depriving him of learning and of growing up. If you want your children to develop into their best selves and have a healthy appreciation for others, you need to let them understand that other people have needs too. For a toddler, this might translate into ignoring her when she throws a tantrum every time you pick up the phone. For an older child, it may mean teaching him not to interrupt when you are in the middle of a conversation. And so on.

- **reign yourself in and let the coaches coach.** In many places, an extraordinary amount of organized sports are at our fingertips, often with a lot of parental involvement. In most instances, coaches are good people who volunteer their time to teach your child how to play a sport. They may not do it your way, or your partner's way, but they are doing it the way they know how. Wasting your precious energy by ranting and raving on the sidelines brings everyone down, especially yourself, and contributes to the problem rather than the solution. If coaching problems remain paramount, parents always have the option of talking to the coach in private or of becoming coaches themselves. Beyond that, it's important to maintain a healthy perspective, cheer on the kids, and let the coaches do their job.

- **at times, accept your child's sadness or anger and don't give advice or try to solve the problem.** We are all upset and hurt at times. These are natural and normal feelings. As a parent, there are times when the best option is to listen and reflect your child's feelings—without giving advice. Your relationship will stay strong if you can be present and listen well, and your kids will gain self-confidence knowing that you trust them to make their own decisions about how to deal with the problem and move on.

- **let your children make mistakes and learn the natural consequences.** Another important life lesson is to learn from the consequences of our mistakes. If your child forgets her homework, for example, resist the temptation to run it over to the school. Let her experience the school's disciplinary actions. She is much more likely to remember her homework next time.

- **life isn't always fair.** We all have experiences that are emotionally painful and unfair in our minds. That is part of life. A learning experience always comes out of these situations. If you help your child and yourself focus on the lesson, rather than the unfairness, you will liberate yourselves to move on with your lives.

- **incorporate other tips in this book to help you lead a balanced life.** You are much less likely to fall victim to overparenting if you take good care of yourself and enjoy fulfilling interests and activities away from your children.

It may be quite a challenge to create a meaningful, fulfilling life for yourself, without being consumed by the inappropriate mommy guilt of our generation. However, by taking a step back and allowing your children to be self-sufficient and learn from their own mistakes —by parenting with healthy boundaries, giving up control in some areas, and including your own needs in the mix—you can do it!

35

the big stuff
for kids

When I stopped seeing my mother with the eyes of a child,
I saw the woman who helped me give birth to myself.

—Nancy Friday

We want our children to be the best they can be—confident, kind, self-aware, able to communicate well with the world around them. We want them to know they are special, unique individuals, yet we want them also to be connected to and respectful of others. As you begin to slow down—to make decisions based on your real values, to prioritize and say no to what is less important—you will notice that you are parenting more authentically. You will rely more on your intuitive wisdom because you've made the space in your life to get in touch with that wisdom. I believe that this is innate in all of us and is likely your best parenting tool.

In addition to what you already know is best for your children, read on for some suggestions to help them live their best life. Consider these tips as friendly reminders as you navigate down the bumpy road of motherhood:

- **promote what they naturally gravitate toward.** If you really observe, you'll notice that your children drift toward certain experiences. Some love sports, some are passionate about music, art, or writing, some liven up when they learn about different cultures, and so on. Build their self-awareness and confidence by doing what you can to encourage their natural strengths and interests.

- **listen to your child.** Try to spend consistent time listening to your children and reflecting how they feel. Don't judge and don't try to change their feelings. Real feelings are always okay (it's the behavior that may be unacceptable). Just listen. Reflect what they are saying. Showing empathy is critical for your relationship and for helping them feel respected, understood, and valued. In turn, they will learn how to empathize with others.

- **teach all family members to share their voices.** There are still many situations when females, especially young girls, all too often shrink into silence. The quickest way your daughter will learn to share her voice, her expression of herself, is by watching you do the same. By refusing to be silent in your family or in your daily life, you are giving her permission to talk just as proudly and loudly as the boys. In some families, sons are also inhibited. Model for all your children, thereby teaching them, that it's admirable to listen well, to share your own opinions, and to discuss issues, even when you don't agree.

- **help them when they're stuck.** When they are really struggling, help your kids think through their options and choose a path to try. Listen to their feedback about how it may or may not have worked out. Discuss the lessons learned.

- **use the same communication principles with your children that you use with adults.** The notion that for kids to learn, they need to be yelled at or lectured is baloney. You want your children to communicate well and respect others, so communicate well with them and show them some respect. That's how they learn it. When they upset you, tell them how you feel. Listen to their perspectives as well. Be willing to negotiate in many situations. By honoring them with good communication and requiring it back, you teach them a priceless skill that will benefit them throughout life.

- **encourage kindness and openness in friendships.** Encourage your kids to play with a broad array of friends. Teach them how to be kind, inclusive, and open to new friendships. Building this character trait, especially in girls, helps them feel secure and also builds a protective barrier against the allures of clique behaviors that rear their head in the adolescent years.

- **respect what your child's behavior is telling you.** I recently observed a mother at a soccer practice chasing her screaming five-year-old around the outskirts of the soccer field and repeatedly carrying him back onto the field. Similarly, my husband Mark and I have felt uncomfortable at times when our seven-year-old daughter prefered to play alone rather than join a group. We've had to fight the urge to drag her into the mix. Sometimes it's best to listen to and respect what our children's behavior is saying. If you catch yourself battling your child to participate in something, your insistence may indicate that you are overly attached to your own beliefs and have lost sight of who your child really is. Take a step back. Respect that your child may—or may not—become interested in a particular activity or group dynamic at a later time.

- **praise their efforts, not just the end results.** When you focus on their effort, kids learn that it is okay to make mistakes. Without this awareness, the fear of losing your approval can prevent them from working at something they don't immediately excel at or from trying something new. Teach them to take risks and to expect bumps along the road.

- **make sure you have realistic developmental expectations.** If you are expecting your toddler never to be sad when you leave or your ten-year-old to want to be with you all the time, your expectations are unrealistic. Don't obsess with parenting books or classes, but do learn enough so that you understand basic developmental stages and can maintain realistic expectations.

- **let your children know that you always love them, even if you don't always love their behavior.** Sometimes you don't like your child's behavior (like when she cozies up to Aunt Ruth to ask her why she's so fat), but that doesn't mean you don't love her. Children need to know that your love is unconditional, without limits and without the need for something in return.

- **keep on showing your affection.** As children get older, sometimes parents mistakenly believe they no longer need affection. They still do, just in different ways. Always tell them you love them, hug them (although, heaven forbid, not in public when they are adolescents). The bedtime ritual may evolve from showering hugs and kisses into a gentle "good night, I love you" as they get older, but don't let it disappear entirely. Showing your love is important throughout their development.

As a balanced mom, you are in touch with your innate wisdom. Add in these tips, as you need them, to help your kids know who they are, feel good about themselves, and interact well with others. This is the big stuff in parenting that's worth your time and attention!

36

what is quality time?

Forget about day camp or mandatory Gymboree. What's the point of raising kids if we don't have a good time and a few laughs?

—Anna Quindlen

If you really want to maintain a close relationship with your children and improve their behavior, this may be the most important chapter you read. Before you focus on discipline techniques, focus on spending quality time together. With younger children, the power of play is amazing. With older kids, interacting in ways you both enjoy promotes a healthy bond between you. The key is to be present and focus your attention entirely on your interaction with your child.

I have worked with many parents who report in amazement that their child's behavior improved dramatically after consistently adding quality time together into their family lives. And, just as important, you will feel better protecting essential time for yourself if you feel safe and secure in your relationship with your child. Nothing contributes to these feelings more than one-on-one, quality time together. Furthermore, by investing in a good relationship with your children when they are young, you are building a bond between you that can help tremendously with the often tumultuous teenage years that lie ahead.

Here are some key points:

- **spend at least twenty to thirty minutes twice a week with each child, age six or younger, individually.** During these playtimes, let your children choose the activity. Give them choices if they aren't initially responsive. Let them be the boss. Observe them and comment on what they are doing, such as "Now you are putting your baby to bed" or "Wow! That Power Ranger is tough!" Dig deep and muster up whatever enthusiasm you can. These playtimes work miracles.

- **spend at least one hour a month with your other children individually.** Most kids over six prefer interactive activities. Let them choose, within reason. (My son would suggest playing chess, whereas my spirited daughter would ask to sing a threesome with Madonna.) The idea is to play together doing something you both enjoy, such as riding bikes together, playing board games, roller blading (yes, you can!). Or, if you both need to decompress, consider taking a walk and talking about your days.

- **your child needs your undivided attention during your time together.** Undivided attention means ignoring the doorbell and the phone (and not listening to the answering machine either). Farm out the other kids, or choose a time when they are either asleep or safely occupied. The world around you will just have to wait. The younger the child, and the more children you have, the more significant this suggestion.

- **ignore any resistance.** Sit with your child and decide what time works best for you both. Children may pretend SpongeBob or their Nintendo are more important than you, but they're really not. Schedule the time anyway.

- **be present.** It's easy to daydream about how barren your food supply is while you pretend to give your child your attention. They know when if you're faking it. In addition, it really is good for you to unwind your brain, let go of the "to do" list, and just enjoy the uniqueness of your child.

- **keep it enjoyable.** I know there are days when you'd rather poke your eyes out than have to play Barbies. That's okay. Perhaps you need to move the time to another day. Or, perhaps you've just had it with Barbies (I know I have!) and need to offer other choices that you both enjoy. The goal is to have fun together, so if the activity closely resembles torture, suggest some other options.

- **keep it simple and flexible.** Quality time does not mean you need to climb the Great Wall of China together. It means one-on-one uninterrupted time together that you both enjoy. Mix it up. Consider going to a play, roller skating at the rink, having a picnic in the backyard, or listening to music at a coffee shop. Get creative.

It's so easy to throw all the kids together (if you have more than one to throw) and to drown in the car pools to endless activities, considering this your "time together." Don't make this mistake. Your child's self-esteem will flourish, as will your relationship, if your child knows you will consistently make time for him alone a priority.

37

the mommy martyr just moved out!

If you want your children to keep their feet on the ground,
put some responsibility on their shoulders.

—Abigail Van Buren

just as we benefit from reaping the rewards of hard work and learning how to function independently, so do our children. When we teach them the tools they need to become self-sufficient, we are giving them wings to fly. Their self-esteem flourishes and they gain an appreciation for the adults in the home as they experience the hard work that is required to manage a household. Furthermore, completing chores together promotes cooperation while giving you both some quality time to nurture your relationship.

In theory, this all sounds great. The problems begin when you actually want your children to complete their chores without starting the next world war. Consider these suggestions:

- **start the process of teaching responsibility early on.** Young children need to know by the time they are two that they are part of a larger world and they need to contribute to make it all function. When they drop their Cheerios, they need to pick them up before you play with them. When they take out toys, they need to put them back before you leave the house. The whole chore system is much easier if you start the process of learning to be responsible early on.

- **oops ... if you forgot to start early, start now!** It's never too late to teach chores and responsibility. It will be more difficult if your kids have a history of not helping around the house, but it's not impossible. Make sure you are especially firm and consistent with the rewards and consequences, and they'll get the hang of it.

- **have a good understanding of what are developmentally appropriate chores.** If you ask your three-year-old to do the dishes, you are paving the way for a disaster. Try to stay somewhere close to these developmental guidelines for most children. Toddlers can put toys and books away, throw trash away, and help dress themselves. Three- to five-year-olds can dress independently, brush teeth (with your supervision), make their beds, keep rooms semi-tidy, and help set and clear the table. Six- to nine-year-olds can feed the pets, take out the trash, put dishes in the dishwasher, help in the yard, help with younger siblings, carry laundry to the washroom, and help sort clothes. Ten- to twelve-year-olds can help or make dinner, do the dishes independently, babysit younger siblings (with an adult nearby), and help with laundry and cleaning the house. Most teenagers, if taught patiently, are capable of doing the same kinds of chores that you do.

- **make a list of chores, dole them out, and post the list.** The list of what's involved to run a household seems endless: buying and putting away groceries, doing and putting away laundry, making beds, keeping rooms picked up enough so you can walk in without endangering your life, and so forth. Make a list of everything you and your spouse do for your family and household and split up the chores with your children. Give them choices where you can. Alternate the chores monthly between children if there are disagreements about who does what. Every child should have at least a few chores they do daily.

- **make some chores a shared event.** Structure it so some chores are completed by a parent and a child together, such as doing laundry or gardening. This creates excellent teaching opportunities as well as some time to connect with each other and talk about what's going on in your lives.

- **have regular family jam sessions.** For fifteen minutes a day, ask every family member to clean up a specific part of the house. Make sure who does what is crystal clear. Then crank some tunes, keep a good attitude yourself, and get going!

- **chores can be rewarded with privileges.** Your children need to participate in chores because they are part of a family. The incentive to complete some chores can be the privileges your children regularly receive. Remind them that they get to watch television, play with friends, play electronic games (whatever they enjoy doing that is allowed in your home) because they help your family function.

- **rewarding some chores with money allows you to teach financial responsibility.** When children grow up and leave their nest, most parents want them to know how to spend money on what they can afford, save some money, and donate some to others in need. Why not instill fiscal responsibility early on? If they don't learn it at home, where will they learn it? At a certain age, most children become interested in making their own money if they need to earn money to buy things they want. A simple suggestion is to pay them monthly, with a certain percentage of the allowance designated to a "spending" envelope and a percentage going to a "saving" envelope. Once a certain amount is saved, you can open a savings account for big purchases. Consider asking your children to donate all of their allowance to a charity of their choice during their birthday month and a major holiday month, when they will be receiving gifts themselves. This is an excellent way to explore charities together and teach them to care. Overall, creating a monetary system to reward some chores is a great way to teach them financial skills that will serve them well in the future.

- **if young children are resistant, start a sticker chart.** A reward system is only effective if it is just that—a reward—in the eyes of your child. For younger children, a sticker system often works. Give them a sticker for each of the three chores that they do daily, and by the end of the week, if they've received all their stars for six of the seven days, they get a reward. Get creative with your kids to determine what is truly rewarding for them. Think about activities you can do together or small rewards they enjoy, like inexpensive books or toys.

- **to keep the motivation strong, tie a refusal to do chores or a bad attitude to a loss of privileges or money.** You want your children to understand that they need to complete their chores pleasantly if they want to be rewarded with privileges or monetary compensation. If you inform them that, with the exception of food, basic clothes, and necessary supplies, they must buy anything they want with their own money, they will be motivated to earn it. If you are serious about removing their privileges if they don't do their chores, they'll be motivated to complete them. Try this system and watch how quickly they catch on!

- **be consistent.** Nothing matters more than your consistency. Consider trading off with your partner to be the gentle enforcer each night and make sure chores were completed appropriately. If you are clear and consistent with your well-thought-out approach, if your chores are developmentally appropriate, and if you effectively tie them to rewards and consequences, your chore system will work.

If you've been a mommy martyr, it's time to retire. Chores are an excellent way to teach your children about important life skills and lessons—acting responsibly, contributing to something bigger than themselves, working hard for things they want, and managing money. Completing some chores as a team gives you a wonderful opportunity to spend time together while working toward a larger purpose. And the help frees you up to enjoy your family more and enjoy some enriching activities on your own. Now, who can argue against the value of that?

38

quiet time for kids

The beaten track does not lead to new pastures.

—Indira Gandhi

now that you are aware of the benefits of quiet time for yourself, why not add this blessing to your children's lives? Wouldn't they benefit from connecting with their inner selves, finding their own creativity, and learning how to think for themselves without being plugged in or structured? If these are life skills you'd like them to develop, consider these tips:

- **build a twenty- to sixty-minute period of quiet time into your children's schedules.** The duration and frequency of time will depend on the age of your child.

Really schedule it! The same time each day can be helpful, such as early morning or before bed. Perhaps you want your quiet time to coincide with theirs?

- **give some guidance.** Tell them that this is their quiet time to do what they want, without television or phones or electronic games. It's time to read, go for a walk, do some art, write in a journal, or get creative in their own way. Make sure some resources, such as age-appropriate books and art materials, are accessible.

- **"I'm bored!"** Fabulous! It's nice to hear because it shows that your kids are really going to have to get creative and look to inner resources, not external allures, to occupy themselves.

- **protect their solitude and let the magic unfold.** Keep the rules clear that television, telephone, and other plugged-in time is off-limits. Keep children separated to ensure real alone time.

- **with toddlers, keep books, blocks, and other quiet activities around, and praise them when they choose to play alone.** With most toddlers, unsupervised quiet time leads to "destroy the house," so skip it. However, by age three, most kids can handle quiet time, semi-alone, in an area where an adult can check on them periodically. Perhaps whoever does the laundry, cleaning, or cooking can get some of these jobs done while your younger child plays nearby for short periods of time. If you praise periods of solitary play and maintain sufficient quality time together, your children will learn to expect, respect, and even enjoy quiet time.

- **a balanced family life helps a child feel secure.** When you include downtime and solitary time in your schedules, your children learn that *being* is just as important as *doing*. They learn that they are okay just as they are, without always having to get somewhere else.

In these quiet moments, your child's authentic self emerges. My ten-year-old son will still play with Legos in his room (don't tell his friends), my seven-year-old daughter creates elaborate dramas with her dolls, and my three-year-old likes to line up her stuffed animals and boss them around. Whatever your child's choices, you are giving your kids the gift of self-expression, creative development, and the ability to think for themselves. Now those are life skills worth developing!

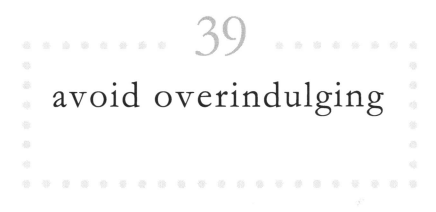

39

avoid overindulging

If we get everything that we want, we will soon
want nothing that we get.

—Vernon Luchies

Children are fortunate when they get to have social time with friends, ample activities to teach and entertain them, and fun toys to occupy their minds. Electronic games, television, iPods, and so on, if given at an appropriate age, don't spoil children in and of themselves. They can be enjoyed as a birthday gift, as a reward for good behavior, or as something the child buys for herself.

Problems arise when children are given whatever they want, whenever they want it. When the scales tip from parent-directed rewards to child-centered demands, and when children's wants are constantly indulged, kids are at risk for being overindulged. They become susceptible to turning into self-absorbed, ungrateful individuals who expect immediate gratification. Many loving, well-intentioned parents are guilty of overindulging their children. Take a step back, get in touch with your values, and don't make this mistake. Consider these tips:

- **think about the appropriate age to give gadgets before you give them.** If your four-year-old wants an expensive electronic game because his nine-year-old cousin has one, is this a good reason to give it to him? Before you succumb to child pressure or peer pressure, think through the development of your child and consider when you believe he is old enough for various high-tech or otherwise expensive gifts. Remember that the sooner you give it, the sooner you might need to monitor the amount of time he spends with it.

- **limit the use of plugged-in time.** Research indicates that many children are watching too much television. What is this doing to their brains? What life experiences and lessons are they missing because they are plugged in for so long? Ask yourself the hard questions and limit the total amount of plugged-in time to a few hours a day. If you need help managing your children, it is far better to hire a creative babysitter than it is to rely on television or electronic games to babysit for hours on end.

- **get clear on family rules.** Sit down with your family and make a list together of the non-negotiable rules. Include the basics, such as "talk calmly about how you feel—don't yell at each other."

- **connect privileges to obeying the rules.** Privileges are the fun activities your child enjoys, such as social time with friends and use of plugged-in time. When the rules are broken, one effective parenting tool is to take away a privilege that your child cares about. What children really care about differs from child to child. Some children, for instance, worship their electronic games and others care much more about their social time with other kids. With this basic tenet, children learn that there are certain rules that must be followed in order to enjoy privileges at home.

- **as they get older, teach the concept that many wants are to be earned.** In between birthdays and holidays, consider asking your child to earn the money they need to buy other items they want (see chapter 37). If you have a large family, you might also want to limit the number of gifts everyone is allowed to give your children.

- **out with the old, in with the new.** Excess at any age leads to boredom and lack of appreciation for what we have. Rise above this problem by rotating your children's toys and/or donating them. As stuff comes in, give stuff away.

Birthdays and holidays are excellent times to encourage your children to donate toys or clothes to charities of their choice.

- **share the gift of gratitude.** Inform your kids that someone else will always have something bigger or better than they do. It's the way it is. If they focus on what they don't have, they will constantly feel like they have the short end of the stick. If, however, they choose to focus on what they do have, they will live a life of abundance.

If you take the time to think through how you want your children to develop, rather than give them gifts or privileges without forethought, you are more likely to guide them in the direction that you want. Avoid overindulging, teach gratitude, and you are bound to have more satisfied, appreciative children in your home.

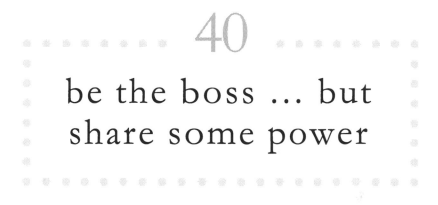

40

be the boss ... but share some power

There are two lasting bequests we can hope to give our children. One of those is roots, the other, wings.

—Hodding Carter

One of the delicate dances of parenting is to make clear that you are the boss yet share enough power so that your children learn to be responsible. By being the boss, you provide the limits and structure that children need to feel safe and secure as they learn important life lessons. By sharing some power and being present to guide your kids, you help them develop self-control and autonomy. Ultimately, if you raise them with a vision toward self-sufficiency and independence, you will dance along just fine.

Here are some tips as you give your kids wings and help them learn to fly:

- **for young children, "no" means no.** Think before you set a limit or say no, because once you do, with young ones, it's best not to change your mind. Once they understand that you really mean no, they are less likely to continue harassing you, knowing that it's just wasted breath.

- **remember to say yes when you can.** It's helpful sometimes to shift the focus from what they can't do to what they can. For a toddler, this may mean giving them a different toy when they want to take away their brother's. For an older child, this may mean telling them they can't have a friend over today, but they can next week. Try to think of how to say yes and eliminate some unnecessary battles.

- **with older children, be willing to negotiate more.** As kids get older, negotiate more of the rules and consequences. Listen to their ideas. They are more likely to respect, abide by, and learn from rules and consequences if they are given some of the power to make them.

- **offer choices.** When you present your child with a choice, you empower her. If she hates taking showers, ask if she'd rather take one before or after dinner. If the kids are driving you nuts with roughhousing, ask if they'd rather play outside or play a quiet board game inside. Often, merely giving a choice is enough to help you keep your cool and redirect your child's energy.

- **share in the decision making when you feel it's appropriate, not when pressured by their misbehavior.** Try not to give into your kids' wishes when they are whining or acting out. Rewarding misbehavior generally promotes more misbehavior and certainly diminishes your authority.

- **allow natural and logical consequences whenever you can.** If your child has a habit of leaving his bike out, take it away for a few days. If she spills her drink, ask her to clean it up. If he breaks television rules, turn the TV off for a few days. By allowing natural consequences, you are taking yourself out of the equation while teaching your children to think for themselves and act responsibly.

- **choose your battles.** Sometimes we lock horns with our children and find ourselves battling more than we'd like. When you find yourself in this position, recognize that you're both expending too much negative energy. Take a step back and breathe. Then identify the one or two problem behaviors in your child, or in yourself, that you'd like to focus on, and let the rest go. For example, you may decide to work on helping your child control her temper while letting go of your obsession with transforming her naturally messy habits into immaculate ones. When you choose your battles, your relationship can still thrive as you manage the big stuff without drowning in all the small stuff.

- apologize when you make mistakes and share the lesson you learned. When you apologize for making a mistake, such as overreacting to a situation, you teach your child that you, too, are fully human. You allow that you are the boss, but you aren't perfect. You show your child that you respect her enough to be humble yourself. By sharing your lesson, such as "next time I'm going to try not to yell," you teach the value of learning from mistakes. In this manner, children internalize the value of apologizing, learning the lesson, and moving on.

Parenting is an excellent opportunity to teach valuable life lessons and to guide your children to become self-sufficient. Keep your eye on the ultimate goal of raising your children to feel good about themselves, to make solid decisions, and to be appropriately independent, so you can live a whole life, and so can they. You want them to be well-equipped to listen to their internal guidance when they are on their own. Guide them along the way, back off at times, and lessen your grip as they get older. And then accept that you (just like me) will make mistakes along the way.

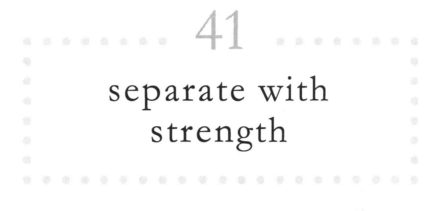

41

separate with strength

Let there be space in your togetherness.

—Kahlil Gibran

encourage your children to become appropriately independent by separating well from an early age. I know that it can be heart wrenching to leave your young children when they are crying and lunging for you as if they'll never see you again. But if you give into this kind of reaction to your departure, it only escalates.

As heartwarming as it may feel when your children really want you around all the time, there will come a point when they desperately want separate lives. In the teenage years, the old "please be with me" becomes "please don't be seen with me." As appalling as that may sound now, it's actually healthy for them to be comfortable in their own skin, without you.

Help them develop their autonomy by being secure in your own autonomy and maintaining periods of separation. Read on for some tips on how to separate with strength:

- **instill periods of separation from early on.** Get them used to the reality that, although you adore them and are willing to make countless sacrifices for them, you also have needs of your own. Even if you are not working outside the home, you'll need time apart to take care of yourself and to pursue some meaningful interests.

- **when it's time for you to separate, do it kindly and firmly.** When they are young, spend a few minutes helping them transition to time without you by interacting with them and the caregiver who will take your place. Then point out what incredibly fun activities are awaiting them in your absence, and go.

- **make sure the caregiver or setting where you leave your child is a good one.** Invest the time and money into finding excellent help for your children. Drop in every now and then to ensure quality care. Look for a nurturing demeanor as well as appropriate discipline. Ideally, other caregivers, including a spouse, will implement parenting practices that are consistent with your own.

- **when you reunite, give young children some focused attention.** Get on the floor and play. Spending ten minutes focusing on them helps them feel safe and secure with your separations.

- **reinforce the bedtime ritual.** If bedtime is rough, consider the following suggestions: 1) Set a consistent bedtime for the week. 2) Give a reminder, fifteen minutes ahead of time, that bedtime is approaching. Let the kids wind down from whatever they are doing. 3) With the little ones, keep a steady routine that may include reading a few books, singing a few songs, tucking in the stuffed animals—whatever it takes. 4) With the older ones, ask them to complete their pre-sleep routines (brushing their teeth, going to the bathroom, and getting on their pajamas) by a certain time, and allow for some extra reading time on their own. 5) Tuck them in. And then when it's time to go, go! Complete the routine within twenty minutes so it doesn't take over your entire evening.

- **if you have a challenging sleeper, allow for one "get out of bed free" pass.** Some children easily adapt to a firm, consistent bedtime ritual. Others will fight it. If you don't nip it in the bud early, you may hear creative dilemmas such as "I'm starving! Do you want me to die of starvation?" for hours on end. Instead, make them a pass they can use one time to get out of bed. When they come to you, inform them that you will handle whatever the horrible problems are (such as the impending risk of malnutrition) tomorrow, and take them back to bed. Eventually, the excitement of getting out of bed dwindles and most kids learn to just go to sleep.

- **consider some incentives.** If it's helpful in your family, choose an incentive for going to sleep and staying in bed through the night, such as a healthy breakfast treat, a quarter for the piggy bank, or a television show they like. Let the kids know that you appreciate it when they go to sleep easily.

- **maintain open communication and consistent periods of quality time together.** Keeping the lines of communication open and interacting together is what keeps you close. As you insist upon periods of separation, make sure that you also make periods of quality interaction a top priority.

Help your children become secure without you. Separate with strength. By maintaining a close relationship, while feeling good about your own need for separation, you can ease any resistance and save yourselves from a lot of heartache.

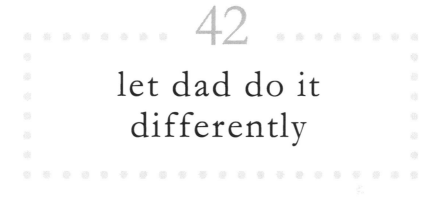

42

let dad do it differently

What too many men (and women) don't realize is that to the extent that women are "better" parents, it's simply because they've had more practice. In fact, the single most important factor in determining the depth of long-term father-child relationships is opportunity.

—Armin Brott

a friend recently recalled the time she left her two children with their father for the day. When she returned in the late afternoon, she was surprised that they were already in their pajamas. When she asked her husband why, he said, "What pajamas?" He hadn't realized that they were wearing their pajamas from the night before, so the kids had worn them to all their outings that day! Thankfully, my friend was wise enough to laugh it off, suppress the haunting images of other mothers shaking their heads, and appreciate the day she had to herself.

If we want to diminish the micro-mommy madness of our generation, we need to be willing to share parenting and let dad do it differently. Yet, at the same time, we know that some parental consistency is important. Consider these tips to help you determine when it's important to let go and let dad do it differently ("dad" can be substituted with any partner in parenting):

- **agree on the general rules of the household and consequences for breaking them.** If you discipline your children for whacking each other and your partner laughs it off, the whacking will continue and you'll be the "mean" parent while your partner is the "fun" one. Consistency with rules and discipline is important. Sit down with your partner at least twice a year to update the rules and discipline. Make sure everyone in the family understands the laws that govern your house.

- **if there are certain areas where you just can't stand the thought of letting him do it his own way, pick your top two or three and do those yourself.** For instance, if your partner is in charge of supervising cleanup with the kids—and, upon completion, you wonder when they are going to start—you may solve a lot of arguments by keeping this job in your domain.

- **try to let your partner do almost everything else his way.** Many of my clients are challenged with this one—as I know I am at times. I was recently frightened by how my husband "fixed" my seven-year-old's hair before they left for an event (think Pippi Longstocking hit by a truck). The problem is, if we insist on feeding the children every meal because "he can't do it right" or we won't let him dress our young ones because he can't match to save his life, we will drown in the family workload and everyone will suffer the repercussions—especially us! (Our brains and bodies can only handle so much. We *are* human.)

- **focus on the strengths of his unique approach, and when you feel like criticizing, zip it!** I know, easier said than done. There are many times that your way really does seem like the better way—to you, at least. But, restrain yourself. Remember the bigger picture: both parents need to bond with their children through effective parenting and time together, and you need nonparenting time to lead a whole life.

Staying aware of the big stuff you want to manage yourself or want to co-parent consistently, and letting go of all the small stuff, will do wonders for yourself, your marriage, and your partner's relationship with your children. What can you let go of this week and let your partner do differently?

43

sibling peace

Siblings are the people we practice on, the people who teach us about fairness and cooperation and kindness and caring—quite often the hard way.

—Pamela Dugdale

i f you have more than one child, you have children who will hopefully be friends for a lifetime. Relationships between siblings can be tremendously loving and supportive. They can also be quite painful at times. Do your best to do what you can to encourage healthy sibling relationships. And know when to back off and let them develop on their own. Here are some suggestions to help guide you:

- **make sure that family rules about how to communicate and treat each other are crystal clear.** Remember that how children learn to treat each other and their parents in the home will greatly influence how they treat others outside the home. Think about how you feel about physical force or screaming as forms of self-expression. If you find these forms of communication unacceptable, outlaw them in your house. Provide a consistent consequence for this type of behavior, such as time-out for a cool down.

- **teach your kids how to disagree.** Wouldn't it be lovely if your kids would always calmly use their words to communicate? Reality is, pigs will fly before kids stop arguing, but you *can* teach them how to disagree fairly. In general, they need to learn how to share their feelings, listen to the other side, and find a compromise or reasonable solution. Sometimes this means taking a break to chill out before he tries to negotiate. It may mean giving into someone else's way, knowing that she will get her turn next time. It may require setting limits, such as "please don't borrow my bike without asking me." Monitor communication, from a distance, and teach your children basic skills of communication that will benefit them throughout their lives (see chapter 30).

- **once they have the skills, intervene only when they are really stuck.** Once they know the skills to work out their problems, let your children use them. Only intervene if the communication is escalating to yelling or physical force. Give them one chance to work it out calmly. If they can't, it's time for separation and a cooldown. Then encourage them to come together again and work it out in a civilized manner.

- **praise them when they are getting along.** Consistently let your kids know that you appreciate it when they play nicely together and get along. Your focus on their positive interactions will go a long way toward their development of a loving relationship with each other.

- **create opportunities for your kids to bond.** If parents are constantly involved in their kids' lives, siblings don't have the chance to bond on their own. Give them opportunities for unstructured, fun time without you.

- **to the best of your ability, treat each child as an individual.** If your approach is to put your children in all the same activities, you may be missing important individual differences. To the best of your ability, with your own need for balance in mind, try to look at your children individually and promote their unique interests. Fewer activities are often better than a lot of activities, especially if they include each child's unique interests.

- **minimize competition and avoid comparisons.** Constant competition can develop into intense rivalry. When you make comparisons, someone ends up with the short end of the stick. Instead, focus on each child's unique strengths.

- **do your best to treat everyone equally, but don't get sucked into their whining about occasional inequities.** It's not possible to treat each child the same, all the time. Sometimes you'll buy one child more than another and you may occasionally buy one child a special gift for good behavior. Just do your best to equalize over the long haul. In the meantime, just say, "I'm not able to always treat you exactly the same, but I do love you all the same." End of discussion.

- **regardless of age differences, encourage interaction.** Special lifetime friendships can arise out of any age differences. Often, personality, temperament, and shared interests will connect siblings in their adult years. During their childhoods, ask your older ones to interact with the youngest ones. Not only does this give them opportunities to bond, it also frees you up to attend to other parts of your life.

- **accept that children who are closer than three school years apart will likely have more conflicts growing up.** In general, if children have the same developmental needs and are competing for the same toys and the same type of attention, there are more opportunities for stress in the household. Only you can decide, if you are blessed with the opportunity to choose, the ideal age differences for your family. But, if you haven't had all your children yet, you might want to think through what you are getting yourself into, before you get yourself into it.

You do play a role in the development of sibling peace—but only to a certain extent. Encourage sibling relationships by appreciating the uniqueness of each child, modeling and teaching effective communication skills, offering sufficient opportunities to connect, and praising when the kids do get along. Then, step aside, accept that some conflict is inevitable, and let them develop as they will.

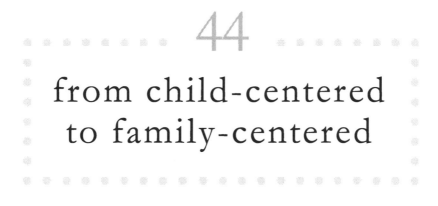

from child-centered
to family-centered

*Don't get so involved in the duties of your life and your
children that you forget the pleasure.*

—Lois Wyse

In our overscheduled, child-centered society, it's easy to lose sight of how important it is to spend time together as a family. And I'm not talking about driving together to the next activity. I'm talking about time to talk to one another and interact. Time to have fun. Time to work together and learn together. Time that bonds you.

Consider these tips on fitting more family time into your busy schedules:

- eat at least three meals a week together. Don't underestimate what you gain from eating together. Ignore the phone and really talk to each other. Ask each other about your days. Play the high-low game where you take turns telling each other about the high point and the low point of each of your days. If one parent generally gets home late for dinner, eat several meals together on the weekend. Get creative if you need to, but get this time in.

- don't let food complaints take over your meals together. If you have picky eaters, give them a few choices when you can. Once the meal starts, make it clear that no complaints are allowed. They need to try everything but don't have to finish what they don't like. If they don't eat, you can save their food for later when they are hungry. It can be a challenge to balance wanting your kids to eat healthy with wanting to enjoy your meal together. Figure out how to avoid the power struggles so you all can enjoy your family mealtimes.

- do something fun together as a family at least once a month. Depending on the age of your kids, ride bikes together, go to a petting zoo, go bowling, take a hike, explore a nearby city, go to the park, go to a lake or pool together—without other families. Have a pizza-and-movie night at home. This is time to have fun together and reconnect. Don't just think about it. Do it!

- **remind your crew that family time is for fun.** Separate family members who aren't participating with good attitudes. Usually a brief time-out improves bad attitudes. Make sure you are also at your best for these times together. (Now that you are living a balanced, fulfilling life, it will likely be easier to feel energized, be content, and enjoy family time together!)

- **make time to talk family business at least once a month.** When your kids are approximately ten years old, it's a good idea to meet as a family to share opinions and feelings about family business. Younger kids can attend the meetings when they reach the designated age. Discuss issues and address problems, such as who does what chore, what the evolving family rules are, and any stumbling blocks that have arisen in your family. This can be a good time to teach your financial values to your kids and monitor how they are managing the money they receive from chores or other jobs.

- **take at least one annual vacation together with your family.** When you vacation together, leaving work and schedules behind, you are much more likely to relax and play together for extended periods of time. Without friends to occupy your children's attention, you focus on each other. You get to interact with each other at your best.

If you've been caught up in the intense child-centered focus of our generation, make the move to become more family-centered.

Make family time a priority and don't settle for anything less. Structure this time in before all the other activities to make sure it really happens. Don't forget that the hours quickly turn into days which turn into years. Before you know it, your children are raised and gone. Make the time to form close relationships with each other and create lasting memories together. You will all be deeply grateful that you did.

in conclusion

If you have worked through this book and put action to your intentions, you will notice that your life is enhanced in some way. Perhaps you feel less crazed and more balanced. Maybe you feel empowered and your decisions are more aligned with your authentic self. Perhaps you realize that your children can still thrive as you focus some of your energy on expanding and challenging yourself. Whatever the change, I urge you to take the time to notice and celebrate your success. And always remember, it's within your power to create and maintain a balanced, fulfilling, and joyful life!